IF DIVORCE IS THE ONLY WAY

'This book becomes a constant counsellor. It provides the emotional lifeline that every man or woman facing a divorce or separation will need' – Margaret Bennett, Principal, Margaret Bennett, Solicitors

'*If Divorce is the Only Way* . . . holds the hands of people in this unhappy predicament. Perhaps the royals should buy a copy each' – Rosemary Carpenter in the *Daily Express*

'A practical and revealing guide through the emotional maze which will be encountered by couples facing divorce. To be forewarned is to be forearmed – if only this book had been available for my journey' – Dorothy Squires, Chair, The National Council for the Divorced and Separated

'It is packed with useful advice, and should be read by anyone who is considering marriage, is married, and, above all, anyone who is considering divorce or going through a divorce' – The Rt. Hon. Lord Justice Swinton Thomas

'This book is serious about marriage. It is not superficial about breakdown; but the author's object is to be readable, lucid and practical about divorce. He succeeds admirably' – The Rt. Revd, The Rt. Hon. Lord Runcie, former Archbishop of Canterbury (1980–1991)

'I commend this book. It meets a very particular need and its wisdom will do much to ease the untying of the matrimonial knot' – The Hon. Mr Justice Johnson, Family Division High Court

'A fascinating look at the pitfalls faced by divorcing couples . . . Straightforward advice about how to avoid the worst excesses, and how to make the best of an inevitably emotional and profoundly disturbing process' – Dr Natasha Burchardt, Consultant Child and Adolescent Psychiatrist

'A straightforward, easy to read and informative guide . . . refreshingly free of jargon. The author writes with understanding and sensitivity' – Jim Howe in *Family Mediation*

'I do commend this book to anybody who is contemplating divorce. It will give them wise counsel' – Raymond Tooth in *In Brief Monthly*

'It promotes the constructive approach that is so important if divorcing couples are to come through the process with dignity and I have no hesitation in recommending it to solicitors and their clients alike' – Nigel Shepherd, Chairman, Solicitors' Family Law Association

'This book addresses the sorry crisis of divorce with a fund of positive advice . . . If the reader follows the path laid out here then the process ahead will be calmer and the burden much lightened' – Dr E. Patrick Reade, General Practitioner

'Mr Bieber's profound experience and wisdom are brought to bear on a difficult subject – with much dignity, compassion and insight . . . A splendid book' – Bruce Mauleverer, QC, Vice-chairman of the International Law Association

'[Mr Bieber's book] will, no doubt, be of great assistance to those divorcing couples who have the good fortune to read it' – Paul Aitchison in the *Family Law Journal*

ABOUT THE AUTHOR

John D. Bieber LL M qualified as a solicitor in 1972. When he merged his thriving practice, it really was so that he could spend more time with his family! A respected international divorce lawyer, John D. Bieber is now a consultant to Margaret Bennett, Solicitors, a highly specialized practice in London, based entirely on matrimonial law. The father of four children, he also writes and publishes, and lives with his family in Sussex.

IF
DIVORCE IS THE
ONLY WAY

JOHN D. BIEBER

AN EMOTIONAL AND PRACTICAL GUIDE
TO THE ESSENTIAL DOS AND DON'TS OF DIVORCE AND
MARITAL BREAKDOWN

PENGUIN BOOKS

PENGUIN BOOKS

Published by the Penguin Group
Penguin Books Ltd, 27 Wrights Lane, London w8 5tz, England
Penguin Books USA Inc., 375 Hudson Street, New York, New York 10014, USA
Penguin Books Australia Ltd, Ringwood, Victoria, Australia
Penguin Books Canada Ltd, 10 Alcorn Avenue, Toronto, Ontario, Canada m4v 3b2
Penguin Books (NZ) Ltd, 182–190 Wairau Road, Auckland 10, New Zealand

Penguin Books Ltd, Registered Offices: Harmondsworth, Middlesex, England

First published by Alma House 1995
Published with additional material in Penguin Books 1997
1 3 5 7 9 10 8 6 4 2

The moral right of the author has been asserted

Typeset in 10.5/13pt Monotype Sabon by
Rowland Phototypesetting Ltd,
Bury St Edmunds, Suffolk
Printed in England by Clays Ltd, St Ives plc

*F*or the children
of divorced families.

*T*his book is offered as a complement
to legal and other professional advice,
not as a substitute.

CONTENTS

FOREWORD

I HAVE WADED through countless books about divorce. Most of them spell out facts competently and offer legal guidelines. John Bieber takes the complex, fraught subject much, much further. This book is philosophical and emotional, as well as practical.

The ending of a relationship is akin to a bereavement. Every divorce is a death – the destruction of love, the pain of loss, the end of hope. Few people emerge triumphant. Even when unworkable and disastrous marriages end, the legacy of divorce usually is guilt, anguish and depression and only a very few people crack open a bottle of the fizzy stuff to celebrate. More often, they open one to try to anaesthetize their memories and blunt their misery.

I am delighted that this book is now published in paperback. It will make it more accessible to the people who desperately need skilled and expert professional advice. These are the people who can't afford huge lawyers' fees, who are scared to walk down the tricky legal path, who need the sensible, practical help John Bieber offers. When warring partners finally walk free to face an uncertain future they will discover, hopefully, that there is life after divorce, provided the divorce is as pain-free as is possible in so painful a situation.

This book, I believe, could help them to find that better life.

Marje Proops OBE

PREFACE

'All happy families are alike but an unhappy family
is unhappy after its own fashion.'

TOLSTOY: *Anna Karenin*

LEO TOLSTOY WROTE with
real feeling. After sharing thirteen children and forty-eight
years of marriage with his wife, Sonia Bers, he left home at
the age of eighty-two. He died a few days later at a remote
railway junction at Astapovo on 20 November 1910.

Today, you don't have to run away from your spouse.
Divorce is available to all. It is indeed a growth industry. It
is also one of the most profound sources of human distress
known to modern society.

The road to divorce is cluttered with faltering marriages,
each at their own particular stage of breakdown. Some people
are emotionally divorced from each other long before they
reach the road, others are not aware that they have embarked
on it; some people work out their problems and turn back,
whilst others live with their difficulties and never reach the
end. The road is well signposted. People believe they know
what it will be like but, if the truth be known, whilst many
set off hopefully few have any idea of how, where or in what
state they will arrive. Making up the flow of traffic each day,
thousands are unprepared for what may be the bumpiest ride
of their lives.

Every year in this country alone, over 350,000 people
divorce each other. At the very least, for each one of them
the experience brings with it disappointment, anger, pain, a
sense of failure and, so often, very much worse. But the

person you are divorcing is the same as the person you married. Is it therefore any wonder that sometimes emotions get in the way and things go horribly wrong?

They don't have to. This book is written to provide you with help at the time you need it most. It is not another legal textbook, although it does cover all the main areas of divorce. It does so from an *emotional* and *practical* point of view. That, after all, is how divorce is endured by those going through it, and the purpose of this book is to guide you through what will surely be one of the most distressing and unsettling chapters of your life.

Written in short easy-to-follow sections, the book takes you through the principal problem areas of divorce with detailed advice as to what you should always do, and what you should try not to do, during the process. Beware, divorce will take over your life. It is therefore essential that you maintain a sense of direction and know where you are going. Divorce needs working at.

This book will show you how a divorce can be managed; how a prior awareness of the problems often encountered, and the mistakes commonly made, can avoid the difficulties that bring to so many emotional ruin; how an understanding of those difficulties, coupled with a balanced perspective and positive attitude of mind, can help you survive your divorce and set you on your way to a more confident and rewarding future.

As a practitioner, I stumbled into divorce work. The sense of fulfilment that I felt in helping my clients to steer around the many pitfalls of the process was almost palpable. My experience embraces several other branches of the law but this was easily the most rewarding.

Never are people more in need of help and guidance than when their world is crashing down about them. It was always a challenge to restore to these people a sense of hope and purpose at what was most definitely their darkest hour.

In divorce and marital breakdown you need all the help you can get. Divorce can be a wretched business. I have tried to describe its many dangers and how to avoid them. If, as a result, you find the process less destructive, I shall be well pleased.

John D. Bieber
Sussex
July 1995

PREFACE
TO THE PENGUIN EDITION

*T*HE REMAINING DAYS of the concept of fault serving as a means to divorce are numbered. Once the Family Law Act 1996 comes into force, fault-based divorce will be banished from the statute-book.

It has therefore been my pleasure to rewrite and retitle chapter 28 as 'Blame is out, responsibility in', in the hope that it will now also be possible to extract fault from the hearts and minds of those involved in divorce and marital breakdown.

Nothing could be more important. For divorce brings with it suffering enough without the *law* obliging couples to add alienation and humiliation to their catalogue of distress, not to mention the additional harm done to children.

When the dust finally settled after the huge debate engendered by the reforms, two great truths stood tall and erect.

One, there is no reason why divorce should not be conducted in a humane and civilized manner; there is advantage to everyone involved that it is. Two, other than in the most exceptional circumstances, no single party to a marriage is ever solely to blame for its breaking down.

If you think about it, these truths are self-evident. However powerful your instincts may be to reject them, consider them carefully. They will provide you with by far the most expedient and positive way forward from what is always going to be a sad and painful period in your life.

'Blame is out, responsibility in', summarizes the net effect of the changes in the law. Not a bad maxim to remember when life gets you down.

With divorce proving such a deeply disorientating experience, I am gratified that many people have found this book to be the lifeline they needed when they were lost.

Let us hope that it will be of similar help to you.

John D. Bieber
Sussex
January 1997

INTRODUCTION

'With this Ring, I thee wed; with my body, I thee worship,
and with my worldly goods I thee endow . . .'

THE BOOK OF COMMON PRAYER, 1552

WHAT IS IT THAT makes the returning of the ring, the ending of the worship, the taking back of the goods, so particularly painful and unpleasant that ordinary, decent, kind and caring people find themselves eaten up by bitterness, greed, anger, jealousy and suspicion; as often as not, the wives turning into Furies, the husbands changing overnight from Jekyll into Hyde?

When it comes, divorce hits the wealthy as surely as the poor, the old as well as the young, the tall, the small, the slim, the fat, the beautiful, the ugly, the good, the bad, the sick, the healthy, even the happy, as often as the sad. A respecter neither of status, class, age, race nor length of marriage, it cuts right through society, picking up and re-arranging thousands upon thousands of lives each year, as if they were no more than children's bricks scattered on the floor.

But divorce is not some sort of virus, striking arbitrarily, destroying marriages at a whim. It is a creation of the law, no more than that, a device for releasing a husband and wife from an unhappy marriage. It is the people who seek divorce, not the other way round.

Divorce has been with us since marriages were first con-tracted. It was part of civilization even in Old Testament days, a fact of life, a humane and, in many ways, an obvious method of releasing two unhappy people from their bonds.

A bond is both a restraining force and a uniting tie. When marriage works it is indeed a desirable existence. When it breaks down and cannot be repaired, there is no more miserable estate on earth . . . except, that is, for so many unfortunate people each year, the divorce itself.

It is perfectly understandable. With the dissolution of marriage comes the ending of a dream, the disposition of much that you have loved and treasured. Everything is reviewed, from the children to the family pet, from your home to your lifestyle and possessions, to the last penny of your income and property. Everything is covered: who should live where and with whom; who should have what; what should be bought, what should be sold. Social workers, estate agents, valuers, lawyers and accountants, may descend on you. All strangers, they are asking intimate questions, making decisions, giving advice; some are even arguing on your behalf. You go through a gamut of emotions, all valid and real. When you married, you probably never thought of bringing in lawyers, yet now you can no longer function, you certainly may not be able to conduct your day-to-day life without them. Disbelief, shock, numbness, guilt, rage, all judgement lost? Sadly, that is divorce.

There is no doubt at all, divorce is a very stressful and sad experience. It can be traumatic, seem like the end of the world, but however ghastly it appears to be, it is only one step on the path through life. After considering the matters dealt with in the following chapters, I hope you may begin to feel that divorce is not the end. In fact, it may just be the beginning of a new, good and wholesome future, no longer soured by past mistakes.

As with marriage, divorce can either make or break you, either succeed or fail. To succeed it has to be worked at. You must ensure that the dissatisfaction, disappointment, sheer unhappiness that have led to the ending of your marriage are cut out of your life and left behind you forever. For that you need some ground rules. If adhered to, they will save you from the consequences of your worst passions, quite possibly from those passions themselves.

You see, there are things that you should try not to do in divorce. There are things, as well, that you should always do.

I shall explain them in this book.

SECTION ONE

❖

IMPORTANT QUESTIONS

'What is the answer?
(On receiving no response) In that case, what is the question?'
GERTRUDE STEIN: last words

DIVORCE IS AN emotional experience. It must be dealt with calmly.

Below is a short table of questions. If you are contemplating a divorce or are already a party to divorce proceedings, then please consider this now, before reading on.

Why am I divorcing or thinking about divorce?

How do I feel about my divorce?

What do I expect the outcome to be?

Why?

Aspects of my divorce that worry me.

What should I aim for after my divorce?

SECTION TWO

❖

GENERAL

1

TRY NOT TO THINK YOU ARE THE FIRST AND ONLY PERSON TO BE DIVORCED

'There is nothing new under the sun.'

ECCLESIASTES

*F*OR EVERY TWO marriages in the United Kingdom there is one divorce. On average each year more than 350,000 people get divorced. If, instead of divorcing, those 350,000 people were to die on the roads, no-one would ever leave their home, let alone go out in a car. If the same 350,000 were suddenly to be taken ill and laid low with a mystery virus, national life would be brought to a standstill, mass panic would become the order of the day. In the United States the figures are well over 2,000,000 a year. The total world-wide would exceed the population of greater London.

Since the early 1970s, the number of marriages registered each year has fallen by over 15%, while the number of divorces has more than doubled. We are witnessing an epidemic. Everyone is vulnerable. It strikes at all strands of society from the most exalted to the most humble. That means that, like you, at any one time hundreds of thousands of men and women are experiencing misery and distress, whilst hundreds of thousands more are going through the agonies that precede divorce. So you are not alone.

It is an astonishing thought that the worst, most painful feelings that you have ever experienced, that you have certainly never before known outside of bereavement, that shred and pummel you all at the same time, should also have been experienced by the woman next door, the man at the garage, your dentist, the midwife, the butcher, your milkman, the man on the television news, your MP, even the children's teacher at school. Suddenly you understand what your aunt went through when you were a child, what your friends have been going through when you comforted them in the past, even some of your children's friends who have been brought home for tea. In one way or another, all of them will have suffered the extremely painful sense of uprooting that summarily changes a whole way of life. The far-reaching consequences of that divorce will affect their emotional well-being and personality. Yet, to all intents and purposes, all of them will have survived.

It is bizarre to think that society can function on such a bedrock of unhappiness but, such is human resilience, it appears that it can. What is more, and has been proved time and again, society can thrive too, despite the turmoil of divorces. For people come back for more. Of all the marriages registered each year, one third are now re-marriages where one or both of the couple have already been divorced!

Being one of a multitude therefore has its comforts. You are not a failure. There is no disgrace, no need to feel there is something wrong with you. You are not the first person to have had their marriage break down when you wanted it to succeed. You are not the only one who has had to deal with the pain and traumas, disillusion and stress. Many other couples have lost their way, grown apart, let each other down, but they have managed to survive as separate individuals. They have built another life and often gone on to find a more substantial happiness than in their failed marriage.

These thoughts will help you, especially at the beginning

when, with everything up in the air, you are confronted with problems or emotions that you have never known before. Far from being able to see your way through to the end, you feel that the world has closed in on you like a forest, a maze from which you may never emerge. You are a lost child who wants to go home but there is no home any more. You have to go on.

These feelings are not unique to you. They are shared each year by millions of people all over the world, being felt somewhere nearby, close to you, every minute of the day and night.

Like you, every one of these people has arrived at a set of crossroads. In varying degrees the direction they now take will affect the well-being and happiness of many others apart from themselves; their spouse, their children, their families, a surprising number of their friends.

It happens all the time. Draw strength from that. Now you are standing at the crossroads. Which way will you go? Make sure you get it right.

2
TRY NOT TO COPY
OTHER PEOPLE'S MISTAKES

'Experience, the name men give to their mistakes.'
OSCAR WILDE: *Vera, or the Nihilists*

IN EMOTIONAL TERMS, divorce may be an essential step to save you from an unhappy marriage but, on its own, it can never even attempt to solve your problems from a personal, family, social or economic point of view. This brings us to the biggest *but* in this book. During those first numbing days whilst you come to terms with your marriage being over, by all means take comfort from the huge number of other people in the same position as yourself BUT, take note, on closer scrutiny their experience may well serve you better as a warning than as an example. The existence of so many other divorces is only half the story.

Here is a list of reactions to the process of divorce. They are all normal, understandable, perfectly legitimate reactions. Do not be afraid to recognize them in yourself. They are the sort of reactions that most people have. Of universal experience, they transcend national, social and cultural differences. Indeed they make up the dress humanity puts on when a marital relationship comes to an end. The world over, these feelings are as much a part of the divorce experience as the filing of the petition itself.

Shock
Uncertainty

Denial of reality
Anger
Sadness
Frustration
Resentment
Bitterness
Fear
Insecurity
Jealousy
Guilt
Hatred
Despair
Loneliness
Anxiety
Self-pity
Self-hate
Sense of failure
Desperation
Rejection
Loss of control
The feeling that your problems have taken you over
Grief.

Consider them for a moment. Apart from the obvious pain which bred them, what do these emotions have in common? Yes, they are all negative, self-destructive, going-nowhere, doing-nothing kind of emotions. Where will they take you? What good will any of them ultimately do? The answer is nowhere and no good.

Now to the other half of the story. The overwhelming truth is that the vast majority of divorcing couples somehow contrive to make a hash of their divorces so that they turn out to be no more successful than their marriages were in the first place!

Why? Because people remain prisoners of their marriage, not letting go of the emotions on that list. They remain immobilized by shock, paralysed by uncertainty. They persist in denying reality. Anger, sadness, frustration and resentment become a way of life. They become bitter, give way to fears and insecurity; jealousy infects their every thought. Guilt creeps in with regard to the children, feeding the hatred that they have developed for their spouse. After a while, as matters drag on, unresolved, and pressures mount each day, despair and loneliness set in, fanned by anxiety. People wallow in self-pity; they hate themselves, they truly believe that they have somehow failed; they are desperate; feeling utterly rejected, convinced that they have lost control of their life, that their problems have completely taken them over, they grieve over wasted years.

Even if you are affected by only a portion of the reactions on this list, how can you take decisions or form judgements, when you have these feelings? How can you make plans or see a future for yourself, when your mind is poisoned? No, comforting though it may be to know that these emotions are shared around the globe, if you are to have any chance of a new life, *you* have to leave them behind.

That is the real lesson to be learned from other people's experience. They get it wrong. A bad divorce and a blighted future are not what life is about. They are not for you. You both deserve and can have something better.

This means learning from other people's mistakes, not just replicating them. Follow the examples that lead to greater happiness. Follow the examples that point to self renewal. Ignore those that lead only to bitterness and sorrow.

It will not be easy. In a very real sense, those emotions on the list quickly become your companions. They are genuinely bad company. Eliminate them. They have to go. Exclude them from your thoughts. Until you do, you will never be over your marriage, let alone your divorce!

It may be very hard. Common sense, logic, even will power may not be enough to shift them. A person does not stop feeling bitter, angry or insecure because they see the self-destructiveness of it. They feel what they feel. Getting rid of negative or troublesome feelings, therefore, means being prepared to go *through* those feelings rather than *around* them by denying they exist.

Most people need a good friend or professional help to put these emotions behind them. Use whatever means you need but be patient with yourself, it will take time.

To help you, I have reproduced the list in Appendix V. To monitor your progress, use the points system that I have included to assess yourself. Being aware of the need to abandon these feelings is a big step in the right direction. Once you have this awareness, you will be surprised at how your determination and the passage of time will see to the rest. In this way, you may not be the first or only person to be divorced but you may turn out to be one of the survivors.

This book will tell you how to get it right.

3

TRY NOT TO BE A PRISONER
OF YOUR PAST

'To bind up the brokenhearted, to proclaim liberty to the captives
and the opening of the prison to them that are bound.'

ISAIAH lx.1

WE READ SO often of inno-
cent men and women being released from prison, their con-
victions having been quashed on appeal, years after having
been sentenced for crimes they did not commit. Have you
ever seriously thought what it must be like for them, once
the bubbles in the champagne and media excitement have
died down?

Consider for a moment the problems of readjustment to
the outside world. They have literally lost years of their lives
whilst the world has moved on. Their spouse, their children,
family and friends have all got on with their own lives, man-
aging without them for years. How can they possibly be
expected to slot back in as if they had never been away? To
imagine their difficulties, just recall the plight of the US
hostages in Tehran. Despite all the good-will and counselling,
the majority ended up with a divorce.

To comprehend the magnitude of their problems, let us
realize how angry and bitter those people must justifiably
feel. They are the victims of a terrible wrong for which they
bear no responsibility, a ghastly mistake that destroyed their
life. Unless they are saints, no lesson can be learnt from the
experience to make life better. There is no comfort. The
wrong done is simply impossible to forgive.

It is hard to conceive of a more tragic situation. Insofar as they have been deprived of their liberty, it is almost unique. However, to the extent that a distressingly large number of people emerge from their divorces feeling much the same way, it is certainly not.

This is no exaggeration.

Too often, divorce makes people into walking wounded. After a broken marriage it is inevitable that one or both of a divorcing couple will experience many of the reactions we have examined already on the list reproduced in Appendix V. At the very least, no-one in that situation will be in a mind to think of anything but their divorce. In an emotional state, they are able to cope with problems only as they are presented to them. Immersed in the divorce and everything that entails, they will have no broader perspective, no thought of how they may emerge from it, of what they will do, how they will feel, of what adjustments will have to be made before they can get on with their lives.

That is perfectly understandable. Eventually, matters will resolve themselves and life will go on for them. Divorce is a very difficult time. However, things can be considerably worse than this. What about those each year who are literally emotionally crippled by the experience of divorce? What about the women in later middle age who have given their lives to support their husbands only to see them depart with their pensions, for a younger version of themselves? What of those who have been battered and abused throughout the marriage and are abandoned when life has passed them by? Or what about the spouses (husbands as well as wives) who have been lied to, cheated, defrauded, bullied, humiliated, made ill, emotionally destroyed? There are all manner of unimaginable hurts and indignities that people can inflict on their partners in marriage, often as the result of drink or drugs. What of those? And, let us not forget, hurts and indignities, overblown because of obsessive jealousy. All these have the same result. 'If you wrong us, shall we not revenge?'

For those, sadly, even if they desire it, divorce is seldom a complete answer. Lacking all direction, confidence, perspective, self-esteem, divorce will often isolate them further, making them feel worse. It is these unfortunate people who can be compared with the innocent prisoner. They may not have been locked up but they are nevertheless prisoners themselves. For them, their divorce is a constant pain, a continuing reopening of all their deepest wounds. All their thoughts, all their anger and passions attendant on their failed marriage remain, even though it no longer exists. They eat, drink and sleep their heartbreak. They sacrifice their future lives either in a passive sense, by depression, or actively, by seeking to cause harm. Either way, they have no thoughts for the future, no emotions save for those of bitterness and hate.

No-one should underestimate the scale of their problems. They are overwhelming to them, their position being infinitely tragic. Yet there may be something, a small point, which may not have been considered before.

Consider this. Prior to divorce, when things are bad and relations fraught, couples sever their affections, withdrawing all intimacy, their minds conceiving of a life without each other. In a word, they become *emotionally divorced*.

But once divorced, what happens to some people? Suddenly, their whole existence is dominated by thoughts of their former spouse. There is nothing they can say, nothing they can do, without thinking of them. In reality they are fighting the same old battles. They become fixated. It is an obsession. Now free to get on with their lives, they act as if they were *emotionally married*.

Think about it. It is a paradox, and all the more intriguing for that, but to identify with this state of mind, perhaps for the first time, may help you to move on.

Rather than proclaim a miracle cure, which does not exist, I would invite anyone who recognizes themselves in these pages to read on. In truth, their problems are really no different from those of anyone else, although being on a desperate scale they are more profound.

There is no future in the past. It is time to let it go. Once that is accepted, these problems can be overcome, even if it takes a little time.

4

ALWAYS BE POSITIVE

'Ah, but a man's reach should exceed his grasp,
Or what's a heaven for?'

ROBERT BROWNING: *Andrea del Sarto*

*I*F I HAD to choose a single maxim for you to retain in the forefront of your mind, it would be this: ALWAYS BE POSITIVE. It should be chiselled in granite or at least placed by your bed, next to the 'phone, kept with you at all times.

For, if ever in your life you need the power of positive thinking, the strength to look to the future, then your divorce is that time.

In terms of pain and stress that it causes, divorce is often compared to bereavement. But with bereavement we can see that, given time, the most devastating grief will eventually mellow, emotions will settle down and life will carry on. It is the same with divorce. The trauma really will pass. Extraordinary as it may seem, your emotions, so deep and confused at the outset, will yet prove to be transient.

After an unhappy marriage, repairs have to be done. Your emotions are battered, feelings hurt, your self-esteem is at an all time low. But you are free. Free to let go of the wreckage of your marriage and, with it, the emotional baggage that you carried with you for so long. Free to take responsibility for your own actions, to make a new life that improves upon the past.

Easily said but words, even fine words, may not alone be enough.

For so many each year, divorce is just a mindless process to get through, a ritual fuelled by ill feelings which must be endured. Regarded as a combat, an extension of the marital battle, it is fought like a final tournament between warring parties. As a result, the process throws up as many new problems as are resolved, destroying relationships for all time. Most people have no expectation of anything better. That is par for the course. Devoid of all imagination and burdened with bad will, this state of mind marks the entirety of what divorce is all about.

But there is more to it than that. Divorce is more than the mechanism, the bare minimum that is required to dissolve a marriage. Pause for a moment. In wisdom, in self-interest, in common sense, should not divorce be capable of delivering a lot more? That it can, that it should, is the key to the way forward. Surely with an understanding of what is at issue, with proper thought, planning and resolve, it should be possible to achieve something better? Of course it is. The result will be as different as black is to white.

Consider divorce as a form of mutual release and you will realize it does not need to be a time of conflict. A release of two lives bound together in marriage, it deserves to be achieved with sensitivity and care, with the least distress, unfairness or rancour. Instead of compounding past mistakes which led to the breakdown of the marriage, efforts should be directed to taking out the hurt, the guilt and all the other negative impulses between the parties. Only then will each be in a position to proceed, for you cannot go forward by re-fighting the past. To go forward you have to feel good about yourself and what you are doing. Achieve that, the exchange of positive for negative emotions, even if it means accommodating factors that you might have preferred to ignore, and you will have every prospect of a wholesome future.

This is the goal to reach for and always keep in mind. We'll call it the REACH TARGET. The REACH TARGET gives you the chance to emerge from divorce stronger and better equipped to cope with life than when you went into it. Ambitious? Certainly. Idealistic? Perhaps. But what is the alternative? What good will it do for you to destroy yourself with bitterness? What advantages are there in being negative? Accept the realities and adjust to them. Give yourself direction, purpose, something to reach for and you'll never look back!

REACH TARGETS must necessarily vary with the facts of each case but there are three essential elements to defining your own:

ONE – Draw a line under the past and learn from it. See where you went wrong. Accept your share of the responsibility. Resolve never to repeat your mistakes, for there to be no more recriminations.

TWO – Understand what you want to get out of your divorce. Freedom, the minimum of conflict, a working relationship with your spouse for the benefit of your children, a chance to live as you choose.

THREE – Feel comfortable with what you are doing in the knowledge that you have not acted unreasonably. The least harm has been done. Everyone remains emotionally intact. You can remember the good times and feel freed from the bad. Disputes have been resolved fairly.

Each of these elements is a goal on its own. These are worth *reaching* for. They will give direction. The past will not have been allowed to destroy the future. You will have conveyed yourself from misery to a brave and fulfilling world.

I know. It's easy to say all this but some people have been so utterly abused they find themselves at the limit of rational control. They cannot cope with the world being dismantled around them, things not going as planned or expected, loved ones letting them down. What of them? How can they possibly feel positive? There will be days for everyone when everything seems to be going wrong. There may be weeks and months of uncertainty and stress, when your emotions are stretched to breaking point. But it is precisely at those times that you have to keep your eyes firmly ahead on the REACH TARGET you have set for yourself. Everything will depend on the strength of your own resolve. Remind yourself of why you are divorcing, even if it's not what you ever wanted, and of what you are going to get out of it.

If you are a reluctant respondent to whom the proceedings have come as a shock and you regard yourself as a victim, then all the more reason for you to try to see your way through it to the other side. Yours is by far the hardest role. The most vulnerable, you quickly hit bottom. But remember, there is no other way to go now but up. Have courage.

Never be deflected from pursuing your goal. Divorce is a time for growing. Define your REACH TARGET and go for it. You will find you have a vision, guts, inner resources that you never before even suspected were yours.

5

NEVER CONSIDER DIVORCE A
PERSONAL FAILURE

'They that sow in tears shall reap in joy.'
PSALMS CXXVI.5

Marriage is one of the most signal experiences in life, certainly one of the most significant and precious of relationships. It is therefore not surprising, when a marriage comes to an end, that people should persuade themselves that they have made a mistake in their choice of partner and consequently have in some way personally failed. We all know that this is wrong but it is very often the most poignant reaction of people involved in divorce.

These feelings are natural for everyone would want to have succeeded in marriage. The frustration of that desire is inevitably a deeply emotional, personal experience, with which we can all sympathize. But where does it lead?

It leads to a choice, which is best taken early on. There is a right way and a wrong way to go.

Either: continue to believe yourself a personal failure who made a terrible mistake,

or: leave all notion of failure and mistake behind and steer your life in a more fulfilling direction.

This may sound obvious but may not appear so clear to those in the early stages of their divorce. Condemning you to a stultified existence, an unfulfilled life, the first alternative is not really an option. If you persist in regarding yourself as a failure, you will act as a failure and eventually you will become one. To continue to believe that your marriage was a mistake will make you afraid of making a similar mistake in the future. You will become over-cautious and un-giving. The result will be an empty, unrewarding life.

The second alternative is plainly to be preferred. Containing, as it does, the promise of a future, it is a liberating, indeed an exciting, departure that enables you to leave your failed marriage and all recriminations and doubts behind. Apart from fine words and resolutions, how is this to be done?

There are several things to establish. As a direct result of your divorce you are going to become a single person again. This means that you are on your own. No-one but you can be responsible for your future happiness. Acknowledge that and you will have taken the first, and for many, the most daunting step. The past is behind you now. You must rely on yourself. That is the *essence* of dealing with a divorce. In a way it is the golden key, the route to fulfilment, to be rid of negative feelings about yourself. Remember, it is only those feelings that have been holding you back. So, let's dispose of them.

It takes two to make a marriage work. In all but the most tragic of cases, it also takes two to make one go wrong. Think that through carefully, applying it to the history of your marriage. Is the breakdown absolutely and only due to your spouse? Did you really have nothing to do with it? Why did it happen anyway? Be honest with yourself, are you really entirely blameless? I am not trying to heap blame on you here, only to make you see that, if you are able to acknowledge some measure of responsibility for the breakdown, a sense of wrong will be extinguished and you will feel a little better.

Remember, both of you may have been hurt. Both of you may have done each other harm as well. Acknowledge that. Try to forgive your spouse. Forgive yourself too! We all have a capacity to hurt as well as to give pleasure. In that, your situation is no different from all other couples who have grown apart. By forgiving the hurt, the hurt will pass.

Finally, try to learn from the divorce experience. Understand that no blame need attach for the marriage collapsing. With hindsight, you will see that, unseen by you, there will have been so many different factors undermining your marriage, all compounding on each other as if determined to grind it down. Learn from that. Instead of thinking in terms of personal failure, think of your divorce as an opportunity to learn where you went wrong. Draw strength from it for the future by making sure that it will never happen to you again. Instead of labelling things as mistakes, accept that there were matters of which you were simply unaware.

In this way you can clear the decks. Even if your attitude is not reciprocated by your spouse, you will find that it has enabled you to come to terms with your divorce. Now you can feel whole again, at peace with yourself for the first time, possibly, in a long while.

Divorce was never regarded as a failure in Biblical times, neither is it now. What would be a failure would be not coming to terms with your divorce, not learning from it for the future. The world out there is waiting for you to rejoin it.

6

ALWAYS KEEP MATTERS IN
PERSPECTIVE

'Love looks not with the eyes, but with the mind.
And therefore is wing'd Cupid painted blind.'

SHAKESPEARE: *A Midsummer Night's Dream*

AND SO WE come to the
second of the things that you must always be absolutely sure
of doing when divorcing. Keep matters in perspective.

Easily said, not so easily done! Issues have a tendency to
grow out of proportion at the best of times. The smallest of
things can assume the greatest of importance. We all have
our flash points and, when these are activated, even the cool-
est and most mature can lose their heads. How much more
likely is this to happen in the context of a divorce when,
for some, just dealing with the process rapidly becomes an
anathema and only the slightest provocation will be needed
for their nerves to snap.

Sometimes, indeed to be fair, quite often, points of contention will arise which will quickly dwarf all other issues,
causing the calmest and most rational of people to
rave with fury. Firm advice, sometimes a stiff drink and,
certainly, sufficient time to reflect, are urgently needed.
Divorce is a time for coming to terms with the unaccept-
able. To survive you must retain your perspective. Measure
everything against your REACH TARGET. Never lose sight
of that.

Yet, as perspective is normally the first casualty of emotion,
it is often quite hard to maintain. For example, how many

among us would cheerfully have the proverbial mother-in-law to live with them?

A short tale from the times of the Book of Proverbs makes my point.

Reuben had always been a reasonable man. Having arrived for a short stay, his wife's mother had eased herself into the routine of the household and showed no sign of going home. She sat in his chair, gave orders to the servants and talked in front of him as if he wasn't there. Even Reuben became exasperated. Eventually, when she was always in the bathroom when he wanted it himself, he could stand no more. He consulted the Rabbi.

'Rabbi, what am I to do? She's completely taken us over. She's there all the time. Never leaves us alone. I can't relax. I can't breathe. I can't bear it any longer!'

The Rabbi reflected.

'You have chickens?' he asked at last. Reuben nodded. 'Move them in!'

Chaos ensued. At first Reuben was sure that the chickens would drive her away, but his mother-in-law seemed to take them in her stride. He gave it a chance but a week later he was back with the Rabbi, a pained and panicked man.

The Rabbi nodded wisely as he listened to Reuben's tale.

'Now the sheep!'

The sheep caused complete havoc. Furniture was ruined, the smell and the din were unbearable, yet still the mother-in-law failed to get the hint. Things were getting worse than ever when Reuben returned to the Rabbi.

'It's unbelievable, Rabbi! Help me!' he shouted. He had taken to shouting above the noise at home. The Rabbi was nodding again as if things were going as planned. If so, Reuben knew nothing about it.

'The cows.'

'What about the cows?'

'Move them in as well!'

Reuben did as the Rabbi said, but within hours he was a broken man.

'Rabbi, what have you made me do? My life is in ruins! The filth! The clucking! The bleating and now the lowing! There's no room any more, mess everywhere and she's still . . .'

The Rabbi cut him short.

'Move them all out.'

That was all he said.

What was the presence of Reuben's mother-in-law compared to living with all those animals? That is the value of PERSPECTIVE. An extreme example, perhaps, but things are seldom as bad or as unbearable as we might think. It is of crucial importance to remember this, as in divorce it is all too often impossible to be both right and happy at the same time.

For so easily issues will explode out of all proportion. If they are not carefully defused, much can be lost in the upheaval. It is not surprising. Divorce is an emotional time and issues, however seemingly irrelevant or petty, have a habit of translating themselves into symbols of hurt and negative feelings. Resentments fast become flags of defiance.

All too often, flag waving defies common sense. Be careful, it may also breach a court order or be against the law. Almost certainly it will run counter to your plans for a smooth and painless divorce.

So again, remember what you are trying to achieve and let nothing jeopardize it. Examine the issues and see if they are real in themselves and of lasting importance. If not and they are threatening your plans, be prepared to back off.

Is it really necessary for you to remove certain plants from the garden? Is it so terrible to return the rug that once belonged to your spouse, or to give up your grandmother-in-law's ring? Is it too much to have your in-laws at a child's birthday party, or, if funds are stretched, to take a bus instead of a taxi?

The answers to these questions may well be 'yes' but put the issues in perspective. Set them against your REACH TARGET, your goal of freedom, of future friendly relations, the well-being of your children, and you will see that they fade into relative insignificance.

These, of course, are only a cross-section of examples, much concerned with in-laws, as many matrimonial problems are. There will be others less easy to discard. Just remember, once fuelled by emotion, the importance attached to issues can spiral out of all proportion, clouding your judgement, even that of your lawyers! The issues will appear to be of importance but seldom will they be matters of lasting substance, for which it is worth risking all that you want to achieve.

Take a step back. A deep breath and remember your positive thinking. Always maintain a perspective. Things will never seem that bad.

SECTION THREE

❖

FACING DIVORCE
AND MARITAL BREAKDOWN

7

TRY NOT TO LET PASSIONS RULE YOUR HEAD

'Let passion be the ship and reason be the rudder.'

DISRAELI

*T*HERE ARE TWO kinds of logic in life. Emotional logic, governing the feelings of the heart, and intellectual logic, providing sound sense to the head. An essential part of the make-up of each one of us, the two are often in conflict.

Whilst emotional logic regularly takes the lead with people falling in love, when they fall out of love, it is essential that intellectual logic should prevail.

With practically all divorces there are bound to be bad feelings. After all, you and your spouse have fallen out of love. You are entitled to feel rejected and angry because your spouse no longer loves you. Your spouse is entitled to feel the same. You have been hurt. Your spouse is the one who hurt you, and this is before you have begun to deal with issues such as the children and finances, let alone one of you having become involved with someone else.

However you imagine you will feel about your divorce, it would be less than human for it not to engender in you some form of intense and painful emotion. You are splitting up from the person you once loved. There are bound to be feelings of disappointment, betrayal, even abandonment. Predictably, these feelings soon develop into those very emotions listed in Appendix V. The feelings may become very intense, reflecting the importance you attached to your marriage. The stronger the feelings, the greater your passions. The only problem is that, in divorce, such passions have to be kept in check.

One of the great ironies of divorce is that, for it to be handled effectively, you must view things without emotion. And yet, as is all too clear, divorce is an emotional experience, probably the most emotional of all the experiences that you will ever have.

Divorce is a big step too. Once taken, your emotions are let out of the bag. Who can say just how long those bitter passions and hurt feelings may have been suppressed? With an end to restraint and a promise of an end to suffering in sight, is it any wonder that some people rush into divorce without much idea of what it is they want to achieve, other than to be freed from an unhappy marriage? Emotional logic wins again.

But it is time for intellectual logic to assert itself. It is time for planning. Important decisions have to be made and you are in the worst emotional state of mind to take them. What are your plans? How will the divorce affect you, your children, family, friends? What sort of relationship will you have with your soon-to-be divorced spouse? What will you feel like? What will happen to your children, your sense of security, your life style, your home? Where will you live, how and with whom? Emotional logic will be of no help here.

Divorce has its own momentum. As it gathers pace, if you are not prepared for it, it will be so easy to get things wrong. You are at your most vulnerable. Feeding off human frailty, misery and distress, the divorce process can often appear like a weapon in your hands with which to settle old scores. It can take you over. In no time you can lose your direction and judgement. You end up repeating all your past mistakes.

DON'T.

Divorce is a new chapter where emotional logic has no place. It has to be very carefully considered, planned in detail. Just as importantly, it has to be controlled. Divorce is a time for maturity, detachment, constructive thought. Regard it as a means to an end. It is no more than that. Let it serve you. Know what it is that you want. Be sure of where you wish to go. Remain calm. Above all, control your passions before they control you. Never has that been more crucial than now.

8

TRY NOT TO SEEK ADVICE FROM
TOO MANY PEOPLE

'Advice is seldom welcome, and those who want it the most,
always like it the least.'

CHESTERFIELD: Letter to his son

'*T*HAT MAN HAS ruined
your life. You must make him pay!'

'Are you sure your solicitor is up to it? It doesn't sound
to me as if he knows what he is doing.'

'Surely you're entitled to half the capital / to stay in the
house / to the car?'

'Of course you have to take the value of the shares into
account.'

'Make sure they don't lumber you with the mortgage
like happened to me.'

'His father's quite well off, why shouldn't that be
relevant?'

'Don't let him see the children until he's agreed to all
you want.'

People do mean well. But there is nothing so unsettling or
demoralizing as receiving contrary advice, particularly when
it is unsolicited.

So often ancient wisdom is best. There is an old tale that
neatly encapsulates the folly of listening to too many
opinions. About a man, a boy and a donkey, of all things,
it is worth repeating:

Walking on either side of a donkey, a man and a boy set off to travel to the town, a good day's journey away.

A hot windless day, they had not been going very long when they were stopped by a woman working in the fields.

'Look at that boy,' she cried to the man. 'All this heat and you're making him walk! Why shouldn't the beast carry him? Put him on the donkey!'

The man didn't argue. The heat was baking and the boy was flushed so he put him on the donkey and they continued on their way. That is, until they reached a mill from where they heard a loud voice booming out at them.

'What is this? The boy on the donkey whilst his father walks? The boy's legs are young,' the miller called from the cool shade by the stream. 'He should walk and let his father ride!'

The boy at once dismounted. The father got on and off they went.

An hour or so later they met a cart coming towards them.

'Are you crazy, in this heat?' the driver laughed as he sped by. 'What's the point of having a donkey if one of you has to walk?'

So the boy joined his father on the donkey. They continued that way until they came to the town.

The day was waning as they arrived. They were pleased to have reached their destination but, passing through the gates, a crowd began to cluster around them. Soon they were surrounded.

'How disgusting! How appalling!' Voices were raised, people were angry. 'Look at that poor donkey, with the two of them on it. It's all in! You've nearly killed it! You should get off and carry the beast!'

That's just what they ended up doing.

The moral? NEVER TAKE ADVICE FROM TOO MANY PEOPLE.

This is important. Divorce is one of the few human experiences which excites curiosity on an almost universal level. As so many people have been exposed to it, either directly or through people they know, it is inevitable that they will offer their opinions and views on all aspects of your affairs, quite possibly touching on considerations that you yourself have not even thought about.

There is nothing wrong with this. Indeed, at a time that will be upsetting and may well be lonely for you, it is reassuring to know that people care. But, and this is a big but, subject to having the right professional advice, with which I deal in SECTION FIVE, only you can decide on whether you wish to divorce and if so how to handle it. It is not for others to influence you in this or to deflect you, however sincere and well-intentioned they may be.

For even with the thousands of divorces each year, no two cases are the same, any more than any two couples are the same. They may have characteristics and trends which are similar but each case has its own fingerprints which make it unique.

Curiously, nothing is more tempting than to follow gratuitous and seemingly independent advice, particularly when it charts a different course from the one you have decided to follow. By all means listen to that advice (though some of it may turn out to be emotional, ignorant, compromised, contradictory, biased or just plain dumb) but make it a rule not to allow yourself to be unsettled or confused by it. If you are, then immediately consult your solicitor who can help you.

For nothing is more upsetting, especially when you are in an emotional or delicate state, than to find yourself knocked off course, or uncertain of where you are going. Nowhere is this more true than with regard to the question of finances which, as the examples at the beginning of this chapter will show, influences most non-professional opinion.

This is not surprising, for the financial settlement on a divorce will often prove to be the most important financial transaction of the parties' lives, determining, as it will, the standard, style and scale of living of the parties themselves and their children, for the predictable future.

Friends and family are understandably concerned. They offer advice, but few, especially the victims themselves of bad conduct, appreciate that in all but the most grave and obvious cases, conduct has nothing to do with the question of finances. In fact, it is all but irrelevant in financial proceedings.

The question of conduct, however, is always an object of fascination to those who know the people involved, inevitably attracting opinions as to how the husband should be taken to the cleaners or the wife cut off without a penny.

Friends and family mean well. By all means look to them for full emotional support, much as you would if you were ill. But, as with any illness where you would leave the medical expertise to the doctors, leave the legal advice to the lawyers. You are paying your solicitor for expert advice. Rely on that.

9

TRY NOT TO TAKE DECISIONS WHEN EMOTIONALLY UPSET

'Marriage is the waste-paper basket of the emotions.'
SIDNEY WEBB

*I*F, AS WITH a husband in the tradition of Islam, it were possible to divorce your spouse by the mere repetition of words, how many marriages would remain intact? For how often in marriage have words been spoken in anger only to be bitterly regretted the next day? Indeed, how often are words like 'I think we ought to separate' really a plea for a positive change within the marriage?

One of the strengths of marriage as an institution, which distinguishes it sharply from mere co-habitation, is the fact that marriage is designed to withstand rows, tantrums, sulks, the throwing of crockery, even the occasional slap (I am not referring to actual violence which may require injunctive relief). Indeed it is said that the remorse and the consequent forgiveness that follow a good row actually strengthen the marriage.

But what if there is an argument – the discovery of an infidelity, the realization of a serious growing apart – and you do not make it up? What if the rage is left to seethe? What if there is more abuse? What if both husband and wife feel themselves wronged by the other?

Such is the breeding ground for divorce and, quite often, as relations go sour, it takes only one further incident for things to come to a head. When they do, emotions boil over and pent-up passions are released. Sometimes the spouse on the receiving end has no idea what has happened or what it is they've done wrong. They listen aghast as the husband or wife announces they have had enough.

That is not the right time to resolve on divorce. Such a decision should never be taken in haste, in temper or lightly. At the very least, there should be a cooling-off period, long enough for the party seeking the divorce to calm down, take advice and *think*.

I'm glad to say that very often people do take professional advice before deciding to divorce. They want to understand their rights, have a broad introduction to the law, simply to take stock before going ahead. This is the correct way to proceed. Divorce can be a devastating experience if handled badly. It is just common sense not to rush into the decision in a state of distress, or on an artificial high. It is just as important not to be rushed into it by others.

It is curious that some people work harder at putting the pieces together after their divorce than they did at making their marriage work. Ask yourself whether the same effort and resolve injected into your marriage might not save it from divorce. Can it be saved? Should it be saved? These are the questions to ask yourself and discuss with your spouse. Be absolutely sure that you understand your own feelings and are interpreting them correctly. Only then will you be certain that you are in a fit emotional state to make a decision and, just as important, that your decision is right.

So wait until you are ready, until you fully understand what you are doing, what you are looking for and how you will proceed. See a solicitor. Seek counselling. Take your time, at all times.

10

TRY NOT TO FORGET WHY
YOU ARE DIVORCING

'What ever sceptic could inquire for;
For every why he had a wherefore.'
SAMUEL BUTLER: *Hudibras*

*T*HE FACT THAT there are so
many divorces each year, and this is a world-wide phenomenon, makes us forget that divorce is the breaking of vows,
the undoing of a marriage contract. It is also the unravelling
of countless personal commitments entered into during the
course of marriage, a reversal of all expectations between
husband and wife. The decision to divorce is an acknowledgement that there is no hope left for the marriage, that
divorce is the only route left for you to find happiness.

It therefore has to have its own integrity. It is not entered
into lightly. A serious matter, it is often disruptive of the
lives of many people. Although some rush into it recklessly,
for others it is an act of courage, taken only after considerable
personal suffering; an acknowledgement that a mistake has
been made, a desire to start afresh, to be free.

This must not be forgotten in the course of proceedings.
When things get rough, bear it in mind. It is pragmatic to
think positively and keep life in perspective, but whilst prag-
matism smooths the path, a belief in the rightness of what
you are doing will ensure you arrive.

This will be of considerable importance when pressures
are brought to bear on you to change your mind, as will
happen at some time from one quarter or another with nearly

every divorce. It is particularly true for those for whom reaching the decision to divorce has been a painful, often an unimaginably brave, decision.

Often, one party to a marriage has been kept in a state of mental subjugation, being abused, beaten and degraded as a way of life. Their condition bears no relation at all to that of most divorcees. It is piteous. It is also tragic as, having no vestige of confidence or self-respect left, they are emotionally dependent on the spouse who systematically oppresses them.

I have seen clients like this. They have come to me and poured out their hearts. They have resolved to break away, to divorce their spouse and start life again. Having glimpsed a new future, they were determined never again to submit to their marital tyranny. They have gone home convinced that at last their suffering is over. They have found the courage to confront their spouse and have fallen right back into their pit of misery. Why? Because, for once, their spouse has been kind. For probably the first and last time in years they have not reacted with fury. They have shown a different side, some warmth, some affection, just what their wretched partner knew once and has craved ever since.

Whether from fear, exhausted strength or some pious hope that all will be right, all thoughts of divorce are put aside.

To people in that desperate state, I would enter a special plea. Remember why you wanted to divorce. You only live once. Take advice and act before life passes you by forever.

11

NEVER BELIEVE THAT DIVORCE
IS THE COMPLETE ANSWER

' "Cheer up, things could get worse."
So I did cheer up and they did get worse.'

JOKE

WE ARE ALL brought up to believe that when the Prince finally rescues his Princess and marries her, they will live happily ever after.

Anyone who has bought this book will already know that this is seldom the case. Almost perversely, the same applies to divorce.

Divorce is no panacea. The simple fact is that there are two people involved in a divorce, the same two people as were involved in the marriage. Even when you are only talking to each other through lawyers, you have to work at it for it to succeed properly. If you don't, divorce can throw up as many problems as the marriage ever did. It is a paradox. Like marriage.

To see why, let me rehearse the things that divorce *is not*. It is not a legalized way of 'bashing' your spouse, of taking revenge, of cleaning out the bank accounts. It is not an automatic end to the distress which you found intolerable in the marriage. Particularly when children are involved, it is not an end of contact with your spouse, not necessarily even with their family. In and of itself it is no guarantee of happiness. The simple truth is that what may have appeared a shining beacon of light in a wretched marriage, may turn out worse to endure than the marriage itself. It all depends on how it is handled.

So what is divorce? I suspect that, in terms of your emotional happiness, it is something more limited than you might have expected. The most helpful and most often used way to illustrate what divorce is, is to think of an explorer stranded in a desert, who has run out of water. His throat parched, his mouth so dry his tongue feels like rope, he dreams of nothing else, convinced that all will be well if only he can find water. Of course he does find water in the end. He drinks to his full, he bathes in it and drinks again, but he is still lost. Finding the water may have kept him alive. It may have enabled him to go on his way. But it did not show him how to get out of the desert. In the same way, divorce may be essential for your emotional well-being. It might enable you to find happiness. But it will not find that happiness for you. Only you can do that.

As with the explorer who realizes, having drunk to his full, that he is still lost, some unpleasant surprises may await you, once you divorce the person whom you blame for your grief. There may well be a period of relief but this could prove temporary. Where will you live? Do there have to be these problems over the children? Why can't the finances be settled the way you want them to be? Why do you keep feeling guilty and sad? Are your friends really avoiding you? What has it got to do with your relatives, what you do with your life? If only your spouse would leave you alone and stop harassing you. Why should it be so hard to form a relationship with someone new? Isn't there more to being free than this? Why are you beginning to feel as if you have exchanged one set of problems for another? These are examples of the kind of difficulties that are most often thrown up by divorce.

It follows, even though the marriage has failed, that every effort should be made to ensure that the divorce works for you. Agree on what can be easily agreed. Set out these points, even if they are petty and obvious, and record them as being agreed. Next agree, so far as is reasonable, all practical arrangements for the children, so that they are able to maintain regular contact with both parents. This, of itself, is of immense importance and, by taking it out of contention, a very real sense of disagreement can be avoided.

Finally, the finances. A common ground of discord, these should obviously be settled sensibly. To help you, remember that in most cases the area of uncertainty, as to how money matters should be resolved, seldom amounts to more than a middle band of 10%. That is the extent of the uncertainty. This means that lawyers will be able to agree on all but the grey area in the middle. That, too, should be recorded. The skill required is then to define the gap and bridge it as amicably as possible.

Seek to emerge from the process with less rancour than you began. Remember your positive thinking. Aim to remain, or even to become, on talking terms with your spouse during the process. If you can do that, you will have had a good divorce. A prize worth working for, it is astonishing how a good divorce can diminish the pain.

Be realistic. Do not plunge into the divorce with false expectations. Enough people have done that with their marriage. Determine what you want to achieve from the divorce and what it is possible to have. With co-operation and moderation, you will get it. The alternative, of a bad divorce, is a war that no-one can win.

So work hard at your divorce. Remember you have to. Be positive. Plan it sensibly and let it work for you. Keep your REACH TARGET in view.

SECTION FOUR

❖

LIVING DIVORCE
AND MARITAL BREAKDOWN

12

TRY NOT TO PUT OFF
TILL TOMORROW WHAT CAN BE
DONE TODAY

'Ah fill the Cup:– what boots it to repeat
How Time is slipping underneath our feet.
Unborn TO-MORROW, and dead YESTERDAY
Why fret about them if TO-DAY be sweet?'

EDWARD FITZGERALD: *Omar Khayyám*

WITH DIVORCE, TODAY is the beginning of the rest of your life. The cell door is open. Outside, tomorrow is waiting. You are free.

Have you noticed how animals do not automatically charge out when the doors of their cages are opened? It is the same with some prisoners when they are released from jail. Freedom means more than being freed from something, the leaving of a situation in which you had felt yourself imprisoned. That is only part of the picture. The rest, the going out, is the freedom to take responsibility for one's own actions and behaviour. There is no-one else to blame now for your unhappiness. No more self-righteousness. You must account to yourself if things go wrong. It is up to you to make your freedom work, to make life an adventure again, to leave past unhappiness behind.

With freedom, life can take off for you, positive things can begin to happen. Only one thing can stop you. Fear. Fear of the unknown, insecurity, even shyness. Failure to think of yourself as a single person, a person of worth.

'The only thing we have to fear is fear itself.' So spoke

President Roosevelt in 1933. His words are just as true for you today. Today is here. Use it.

All too often now, when people are trying to be positive, todays belong to yesterdays, when they should be with tomorrow. For it is all very well dreaming of a future but you have to work hard to have the one you want. It is no good just wishing for it. Every day has to be another step towards your goal. It must not be wasted.

Divorce provides both means and opportunity for you to find a new tomorrow. What better time for you to start your search than right now, today? And yet, you would be amazed at how, in the first few days and weeks of proceedings, so many people rush like lemmings, to some form of personal disaster. In this section I have tried to identify those areas where people mostly go wrong. It is such a difficult, disorientating time, it is no wonder. Depression, hysterics, alcoholism, even suicide, are not uncommon. People do not appreciate how devastating the process can become when pursued without adequate thought or guidance.

Take today to consider your own position. Read the headings which follow carefully. They are written for you. Check the progress of your own divorce against them. Use them to chart your course for they highlight traps and holes that are best avoided if you are to claim a good future.

13

TRY NOT TO GIVE IN TO
SELF-PITY

'Pity is but one remove from love.'
SAMUEL RICHARDSON: *Sir Charles Grandison*

'WHERE DOES IT say I have to be fair?'

In Joseph Heller's delicious book *God Knows*, that response is imputed to God on being asked whether something was fair.

Not a bad answer. Life, particularly in divorce, can seem terribly unfair but no-one was ever promised anything else.

Of course, to a very large extent, though not entirely, life is what you make of it. If you remain locked in your marriage, unable to let go of the past, you will never move forward. If you still regard yourself as part of a couple rather than as a single person, you will never have a sense of your own value or worth.

In time you will find that there are many things about which you can be sorry for yourself. Self-pity will become a way of life. Perceiving yourself as a victim, you will become one. A victim of yourself though, of your own shortcomings, not of your divorce. Unable to accept a share of the responsibility for your marriage break-up, or to cope with your new life, you will end up on a barren, self-destructive road.

Life changes. Life moves on. You must find yourself in the new divorced person you have become, or life will go on without you. By all means feel sorry for yourself at first.

Who has not felt sorry for themselves at some stage of their lives?

It is inevitable in a divorce but self-pity is an indulgence and, like all indulgences, it can be taken too far.

For, unlike bitterness, fury, jealousy, hate, all emotions which are directed at someone else and yet will probably still end up hurting you, with self-pity you take the full force. It is turned on no-one but yourself.

At first it is most seductive, a comfort like a glass of fine brandy. But it is addictive too. Soon you will need more than a glass, a whole bottle. As you take more, you will lose sight of reality. Your attitudes will change, your self-confidence will be eaten up, you will lose your self-esteem, all sight of the real you.

You will believe that you are no more responsible for the misery of your situation than you would be if a tree had fallen across your car in a storm. Convinced that you are hard done by, that life is unfair, you will come to regard yourself as a failure, casting around for others to blame. You will blame them for everything, even for things that happened before you and your spouse ever met.

Self-pity attaches to you, corrupting your judgement, distorting the truth. It is regressive, inimical to positive thinking, to any thinking at all which involves anyone but you.

No good ever comes of it.

14
TRY NOT TO DO
ANYTHING DESPERATE

'It is a characteristic of wisdom not to do desperate things.'
HENRY DAVID THOREAU

IT WAS THE last straw that broke the camel's back. While human beings can often show tremendous resilience in the most terrible of situations, even the toughest can snap. Who can say what that last straw might be?

I have included in Appendix I a list of useful names, addresses and telephone numbers for anyone who needs them but you should remember that just talking, to a friend, to parents, a GP, is in itself a safety valve, a means of reducing the pressure when things get bad.

Who knows what degree of stress a person can take, or when one more upset will shift the balance of their mind? It takes only one tragedy for everyone to see that no divorce, nothing, is worth anything against the value of a single life. It is up to you to bear this in mind, particularly if there are any warning signs; for example, that your spouse is exceptionally distressed or pitifully vulnerable under strain. Don't push them too far. It is not necessary.

It will not be just the shock or despair of the divorce which causes someone to take their own life. It will be those things, coupled with the complete absence of expectation, the abandonment of all hope, the seeming inability to go either back or forward, that will push a person over the edge.

It is when people feel locked into fear and uncertainty, unable to take responsibility for the shape of their own life, that the future appears so terrifyingly fraught. Quite possibly, they have never had to take decisions before and now they are alone and must determine what they want and will do with their life. It is their choice. No-one can tell them what to do. Yet trapped in fear, they stand immobilized like a rabbit caught in the headlamps, detached, curiously disengaged from life. Empty, defeated, incapacitated, helpless, they remain frozen, abdicating all forms of decision even as to the smallest things like getting out of bed. These are the warning signs. Sliding deeper into apathy, it is not that far from there to suicide.

For those under stress, you must also try to maintain a perspective. Even at your very lowest ebb, you have the strength to help yourself. Human beings are made that way. Nothing is as bad as it may seem. Indeed, there will always be others whose situation is worse than your own. Remember, you too have obligations, particularly to your children. None of them will be better off without you, whatever you may think.

If things spin out of control, get help. Someone *will* help you. And time will heal. It always does. One day you'll be glad that you're still there to enjoy it.

15

TRY NOT TO BE VINDICTIVE

'Whom God would destroy He first sends mad.'

JAMES DUPORT

*I*N NO OTHER form of human relations does such scope exist for two people to cause each other harm. With divorce the gloves are off. When faced with rejection some people need to retaliate. After years of suffering a loveless marriage, it can appear to some like a licence to attack, to settle old scores, an overdue and legitimate way of getting their own back.

And so . . .
new Mercedes are driven into swimming pools . . .
vicious slanders are uttered . . .
wardrobes of designer clothes are slashed . . .
business records and papers are burned . . .
personal possessions disappear . . .
cellars of wine are poured or given away . . .
family functions are ruined . . .
new relationships are undermined . . .

The list is endless.

I had a client who was on his fourth marriage. His second wife had managed to destroy his third marriage and, before my eyes, I could see her succeeding in her efforts to undermine the fourth. Hate? Love? In passionate relationships the two are so close, hate seems like love's footprint when love goes away.

'Heav'n has no rage, like love to hatred turn'd,
Nor Hell a fury, like a woman scorn'd.'

With rejection comes a passion many times more powerful than any love shown in the relationship, accompanied, as often as not, by a lust for revenge.

These feelings are as old as love itself. Francis Bacon summed it up when he wrote: 'Revenge is a kind of wild justice, which the more man's nature runs to, the more ought law to weed it out.'

Swift, effective, almost guaranteed of impact, with often devastating results, wild justice is precisely the kind of justice that people seek when they are rejected and hurting; but so often, it is not the kind of justice allowed for by law.

We've all heard of and enjoy reading about cases where one spouse exacts revenge (or wild justice) against the other. Seeking vengeance against your soon-to-be-ex-spouse may be all very amusing to others but, at the end of the day, it is really no more than a form of self-abuse. Certain to lead to tears, it will inevitably rebound on the perpetrator, because the law does not exist for people to take into their own hands like vigilantes. We do not live in a jungle or a frontier town. The tabloids may have a field day but the Courts take a dim view of people who seek revenge.

Venom, fury and hysteria, therefore, can only be tolerated in small doses. If tempted to increase the dose: DON'T!

16

TRY NOT TO DENY THE GOOD THAT WENT BEFORE

'The evil that men do lives after them,
The good is oft interred with their bones.'

SHAKESPEARE: *Julius Caesar*

I WAS GIVEN A draft once of a letter it was proposed I should send to a cheating husband, accusing him, among other things, of ruining his wife emotionally, physically and financially. The letter had been prepared by her father, as a father, even though he was a senior lawyer. Written in anger, the letter held the husband entirely to blame for the breakdown of the marriage. In doing so, it denied that the marriage had ever been of merit or value. This was wrong. There were two children, both well-adjusted, and the wife, who showed no sign of abuse, was perfectly all right.

We decided such a letter would not help. The divorce went ahead on an amicable basis and the least harm was done to a family of four.

It is inevitable that there will be bad feeling on a divorce. It would be unusual if there were not. Afterwards, it is tempting to bury the whole marriage experience in an effort to put it behind you. It's only human. But divorce exists to bring marriage to an end, not to say it never happened.

We are the products of our own experience. To deny this, diminishes us and the people with whom we have shared our lives, including the children.

Of course there were good times, even if we only remember the bad. Do not deny them. Take out the facts and examine them. Feel comfortable with them. Only then will you be able to move on to your new life.

In doing so, you will have learned from your marriage rather than writing it off as a mistake. Your marriage will always be a part of you. If you did make mistakes – and who has not? – you can look back to identify what went wrong. You can acknowledge your bad judgement, your lack of understanding, the clumsy way you maybe handled problems. Analysing your mistakes, you will find a more developed person, better able to deal with life's problems in future. What is more, confronted with your share of the responsibility for the marriage breakdown, you will find it much more easy to take a rational view of any dealings with your spouse.

By being honest with yourself and critical in this way, the positive aspects of your marriage will come into focus. You will see that those years were by no means a waste of time. On the contrary, they prove your capacity to love, and care, be kind, patient, concerned like anyone else; to share, to enjoy companionship, raise a family, to survive. All essential qualities which will remain with you in future life and help you form new relationships.

Human feelings are endlessly complicated but, if programmed correctly, they will get you through your divorce. One of the secrets is to be open and honest with yourself. As, by moving a single letter, UNITE becomes UNTIE, so, by not denying the good things about your marriage and yourself, you will take all that is best with you into single life.

17

NEVER BE INTIMIDATED,
NEVER GIVE IN TO GUILT

'The truth is on the move and nothing can stop her now.'

ÉMILE ZOLA

THE VERY PEOPLE who make your life unbearable in marriage – your spouse, in-laws, your spouse's friends – will quite often be the very people who throw up their hands in horror at your decision to seek a divorce and will do their utmost to persuade you to give up.

The pressures can be very considerable, particularly if your spouse changes behaviour and starts being nice to you.

This is where guilt comes into play. All the factors that made your decision to divorce so difficult are brought up again. The effect of the divorce on your children, the hurt to your spouse, the worry about what it will do to your parents, how it will break up the family, life will never be the same . . . Promises will be made that your spouse will try harder. Inducements will be offered, holidays, trial periods to persuade you that everything will be all right. You will feel unsettled. Your self-confidence will go. You may lose faith in the conviction that your decision is right. The prospect of a single life may suddenly not seem so good. Your mind goes back to why you wanted to divorce. All the thinking that led to the decision is still valid. So is your pain. You are confused. You need time to think.

Remember the two kinds of logic, that in divorce the logic

of the head must prevail over the logic of the heart? The difference on this issue is significant and can be very marked.

The logic of the heart says: 'If I divorce my spouse, I'll break up the family. I'll disrupt everybody's life. The children will never be the same, quite possibly they'll grow up to hate me. What is more I'll break my spouse's heart.'

However, the logic of the head has a totally different, an alternative, more detached view. 'Guilt is inevitable in divorce but it cannot rest on only one pair of shoulders. Divorce is the consequence of a marriage not working out. For that, both parties must share the responsibility. If there is guilt, therefore, it is because the marriage has failed. All other considerations stem from that.'

Guilt can be very destructive. It can be used as a weapon and it can lead to the wrong decisions, especially in relation to your children, either by causing you to deny the existence of problems, or to over-compensate for them. It can also be used constructively. It can help you to focus on your children's problems, regarding them as a challenge to be resolved in a positive fashion. Similarly, you can use it to ensure that your divorce goes ahead as smoothly as possible.

By concentrating on the constructive side of guilt, you can keep matters in perspective. If both you and your spouse are responsible for the failure of your marriage, it follows that you are both responsible for the consequences. Accordingly, you should work together to ensure that as much as possible is agreed between you, particularly with regard to the children. If you are able to agree your REACH TARGETS and help each other attain them, you will find that your admission of guilt will provide the impetus needed to avoid conflict and unnecessary further pain.

But all of this is a long way from where we started. It takes a deal of courage to bring a marriage to an end. It requires a large amount of thought and planning also but, unless it is really a cry for help, your decision, if taken for all the right reasons, should not be lightly set aside.

As the title to this book will show, divorce, to my mind, is appropriate *only* if there is no other way. But if, after taking relevant professional advice, considering the possibility of reconciliation and understanding the full implications of what you are doing, you still want a divorce, it would be very unfortunate if you allowed yourself to be intimidated.

Having suffered long enough to want to end your marriage, you have to think of you. By all means take further advice and consider your options very carefully indeed but, unless there is some new or overwhelming possibility of finding happiness in your marriage, do not be pressured into giving up.

Above all, do not give in to guilt by allowing yourself to be persuaded that you are behaving badly or doing wrong in seeking a divorce. Do not allow problems and difficulties thrown in your path to change your mind. Divorce is seldom easy but it is conducted according to a system of rules. Use the system and you will not be abused.

Take strength and comfort from your friends. Keep your sights firmly on your REACH TARGET. Do not look back.

18

TRY NOT TO PUT YOURSELF IN AN UNTENABLE POSITION: NEVER BEAT YOUR HEAD AGAINST A BRICK WALL

'When men understand what each other mean, they see, for the most part, that controversy is either superfluous or hopeless.'

CARDINAL NEWMAN, 1839

ALL AREAS OF disagreement in divorce have an emotive potential. The danger of trying to reconcile conflicting claims and points of view is that people do not always find it easy to recognize what is a reasonable position, nor necessarily even to understand one after it has been professionally explained. The most bitter and lasting harm can therefore be done with both sides convinced that they are right and the other is wrong, and nothing anyone says to the contrary will persuade them that this is not so.

In many cases one can see people heading for a fall, particularly when disputes concern children who cannot be divided up like items of property, although, in a few instances, the application of King Solomon's sword might well produce different results.

A couple of examples will reveal a little more. These facts are common to both cases:

As far as the husband was concerned, there was nothing wrong with his marriage. The wife looked after the children. She did not work. The husband had his own business and the family lived well. They had a desirable house, two cars, holidays abroad, and the children were down for private schools. The wife took up with another man and filed for divorce on the grounds of her husband's behaviour, citing his obsession with work which meant she hardly ever saw him.

In one case, the wife's new man was younger than she was, and unemployed. The husband had enough funds to rehouse himself without selling the matrimonial home. He was therefore ordered to leave it: the other man moved in: the wife kept the children.

In the other case, the wife's new man was Greek. She left England to live with him in Athens. The Court allowed her to take the children with her.

Neither case is that uncommon. They were decided in this way as young children are deemed to be better off with their mother.

From both husbands' point of view, the orders made in these cases must have been very bitter pills indeed to swallow. And yet any experienced matrimonial lawyer would have advised that these results were inevitable. The law can be harsh. It can certainly appear to be so.

Having said that, there is no point in refusing to accept it. If parties in similar cases can be helped to understand their position, it is to be hoped that they will also appreciate the folly, on both emotional and, it must be said, financial grounds, of beating their head against a brick wall.

The same considerations apply to financial claims where factors other than ownership come into play. As we saw in the first case, the husband lost his home. In many instances, parties persist in making extravagant claims which are ultimately thrown out. Their position is seen to be untenable and yet, spurred on by vindictiveness, greed or spite, and against all advice, they have their day in court – and, all too often, years in which to regret it.

I wonder sometimes whether Trial by Ordeal was such a bad thing! What is certain is that the more reasonable you are, the less scope there is for grief. There will always be hard cases – who can ever really get over losing their children? – but with goodwill and a constructive approach, even the impact of these can be mellowed.

19

TRY NOT TO FORGET
THAT JUDGES ARE HUMAN

'Consider what you think justice requires, and decide accordingly.
But never give your reasons; for your judgement will probably be right,
but your reasons will certainly be wrong.'

EARL OF MANSFIELD: *Campbell's Lives of the Chief Justices*, 1874

As far as I know, I am the
only English lawyer ever to have addressed the High Court
in the Kingdom of Bhutan. Bhutan is a small country hidden
away in the Himalayas to the north-east of India, ruled by a
good king. Very remote and almost feudal, it remains largely
undeveloped. To reach the High Court in Thimpu, some
people will have had to walk four or five days before finding
a road to take them to the capital. In some far flung areas,
the wives have four husbands. The king has four wives (all
sisters) but, intriguing though that may be, that is not the
point of my referring to this beguiling country. What I want
to tell you is that it has no lawyers!

Not one! And yet the judges dispense justice and the law
is respected without the wearing of wigs or the charging of
huge fees or the need to have experts to advise on the law.
There is a sort of innocence to the system, where each party
represents themselves. The panel of five judges tell from
observation who is speaking the truth and their experience
determines how justice should be done. Theirs is the highest
court. From them, appeals go straight to the King.

Can you imagine that system in our own country? It would
not work but, at the end of the day, once you have sweated

through solicitors and barristers, accountants, social workers, correspondence, reports, pleadings, affidavits and delays, you still only get to a judge. Not an oracle, not even a computer capable of making an absolute ruling on the press of a button. Just a human being. Expert, trained, experienced, but just as stressed, overworked, harassed, just as susceptible to domestic problems and, yes, just as fallible as the rest of us.

Remember this when insisting on your case going to trial. No lawyer will ever give you 100% odds on success, even if your case is cast iron. This is because the judge may be fickle, he may have had a row with his wife, he may be off-colour from something he ate last night, someone may have dented his car. Anything and everything may affect his judgement, just as it would yours.

I had experience of this with a judge who seemed to have a bias in favour of wives. I won my first case, about which there were doubts, and lost my next the following week, even though we were confident of winning. The wife was delighted in the first case. In the second, for the husband, we had to go to appeal to have the judgement reversed.

Considerations and experiences such as these add to the pressure of claims being settled. There is a wisdom in that too, apart from avoiding the risk of litigation. Costs are saved, confrontation avoided. There are no winners or losers.

In Bhutan, the case that I watched concerned a dispute about land between a man and a woman. The litigants, representing themselves, were bare-foot and, at all times, the man kept his head down, his eyes below the level of the dais on which the judges were sitting. He was holding his shawl, which all males have to wear on official occasions, in a hand stretched out before him in supplication.

I mention this in contrast to our own system, where

witnesses are coached not only on how to give evidence, how to dress, to project their voices, but also on their demeanour and generally how to impress the judge. Perhaps we should not be hard on our judges. Remember they are human.

20

TRY NOT TO LEAVE
MATTERS UNTIDY

'What is Matter? – Never mind.
What is Mind? – No matter.'

Punch, 1855

ON A PRACTICAL level, things have to be done after a divorce that the lawyer may consider obvious and therefore may not remind you to do.

Everything in joint names should be separated:

Building Society and bank accounts
Burial arrangements
Covenants
Credit cards
Documents of title
Hire Purchase, Leasing, Rental agreements
Insurance (home, car, health)
Maintenance contracts (TV, video, appliances, machinery etc.)
Memberships (AA/RAC, National Trust, galleries, discount associations, sports clubs, other clubs, family memberships)
Mortgages
Residents' or other parking facilities
Service charges
Store accounts
Subscriptions

Unless agreed otherwise, guarantees should be cancelled and, most importantly, each party should make a new will. You will probably have already advised your children's schools about your matrimonial problems. They should be told of the divorce and made aware of any matter causing undue distress to a child.

Each party is on their own after a divorce. They should therefore have their own advisers and access to whatever help or services they may need in life, independent of their former partner. Your solicitor will probably be in a position to provide introductions to a number of accountants, insurance brokers or other professional help you may need, for you to make your choice.

Much distress can be avoided if these matters are dealt with as a matter of course during the process of the divorce. From the grotesque to the embarrassing, no end of upset may arise if they are overlooked.

In an extreme case, former spouses who hated the very sight of each other, may find themselves sharing eternity together in adjoining graves; liabilities may be incurred by one party which the other will be asked to settle; matters such as spending on credit cards or charge cards which are private to one party may be revealed to the other; it may prove impossible to operate bank or building society accounts or to dispose of property without the co-operation and signature of your former spouse.

With the same professional advisers, including doctors, you will never feel entirely confident that your most personal affairs are indeed wholly private and separate from those of your former husband or wife.

Make a list and consider it over a period. You will be surprised how many things ought to be separated, and may be overlooked. All part of the process of being divorced and leading independent, separate lives, this practical aspect is a key factor in helping you to feel comfortable as a single person, ready to face and cope with the future.

SECTION FIVE

❖

REPRESENTATION

21

NEVER HAVE AN INEXPERIENCED OR INCOMPETENT LAWYER TO REPRESENT YOU

'The first thing we do, let's kill all the lawyers.'
SHAKESPEARE: *King Henry VI, Part II*

*I*F YOU WERE struck down by toothache, you would expect to go to a dentist. If you needed surgery, you would go to a surgeon. If you needed psychiatric help, you would go to a psychiatrist.

So why, with a divorce, potentially the most towering problem of your life, should you choose for a solicitor anyone other than a specialist in the field? There is no point in going to the firm who handled the conveyancing, when you bought your home, if they do not have the expertise you require. Being cheap, local, or convenient, is not enough, nor is being a family friend. The most devious circles can quite legitimately be skated around solicitors who do not know their law or procedures or what they should be doing. Were they doctors and you their patient, you would lose limbs or even your life, due to their inexperience. It is up to you. There is no excuse for not seeking the best help available, especially as this can be obtained on Legal Aid.

Advice as to where to find appropriate help is available through Citizens' Advice Bureaux, the Law Society, the Solicitors' Family Law Association and divorce support groups. Even *Tatler* has published a feature on expert firms. But the best and most reliable introduction will be by personal recommendation. So many people have had matrimonial problems and divorces. There is no substitute for making proper inquiries as to whom they consider the best.

The best will be the person who is best for you. Solicitors come in all shapes, ages and sizes. You may prefer a woman, you may want a man. You may want someone of your own age and background, you may be much happier with someone older. Make a list of suitable candidates within a radius which you could comfortably travel, and see them all. Interview them, select the one you prefer and find you can most easily talk to, who puts you at ease and helps you relax.

This is so important. You should be able to discuss what it is that you want out of your divorce. An experienced solicitor will help you to focus on what is important and listen sympathetically to those aspects which are causing you particular concern.

You may be in a state of confusion, not knowing what it is that you want. Perhaps you will not be able to define your own problems and they will have to do it for you.

Do not worry. They will not assume that you have any knowledge of the law. They will explain things to you clearly and without the use of jargon so that you may understand what they can do for you, and what will be happening once they represent you. This will greatly assist you when, having a proper grasp of the issues, you come to formulate your REACH TARGET. You will then appreciate how important that is. Only then will an overall strategy emerge for the handling of your divorce.

Your strategy means the tactics to be employed for the conduct of your divorce. It should be agreed with your solicitor and then closely adhered to. At this stage you must be satisfied that the strategy will enable you to realize your REACH TARGET and that, dealing with your spouse's solicitors on your behalf, your solicitor is the right person to put that strategy into effect.

So much can be achieved by striking the right note with the other side, even with the first letter, whilst the wrong approach can rock the boat, jeopardizing all your plans. There is no point in retaining a belligerent solicitor, who will rub everyone up the wrong way, if your case needs a sensitive hand on the tiller. Equally, if you need to make a big impact to sort things out, it would be senseless retaining an essentially mild adviser.

Your solicitor will become a major figure in your life for as long as the proceedings last. It is desirable, therefore, that you are comfortable with them as an individual, for you will be relying on their experience and trusting to their judgement. However, do not forget that they are only lawyers. They are human. They are neither therapists nor confessors.

However busy they are, your solicitor should be able to make time for you and not push you onto someone else to deal with, although on those occasions when they are in court or in meetings it will be helpful to be able to speak to an assistant in their absence.

They should clearly explain their basis of charging and strive to keep costs down. You should maintain confidence in their ability and feel free, at all times, to ask them to explain matters that you do not understand. They should be candid with you, anticipating questions that you may be afraid to ask. They should keep you up to date on everything, advising you clearly as to the implications of all developments. It always helps to have copies of relevant letters and documents which your solicitor should provide as a matter of course.

Whilst your solicitors must make you believe that they care and are on your side, they must also be able to advise you of things that you may not wish to hear. They must be able to be as tough with you as with the other side.

Now you can see why just anyone will not do. There may never be a matter that is more important to you than your divorce. Mistakes can exact a terrible toll in emotional, family and financial terms. A high degree of responsibility is therefore required, coupled with a considerable degree of skill, if problems are to be avoided.

A solicitor has to advise you on your whole position, your obligations, entitlements and how you should proceed. They have to give you support and perspective in what for you is an emotional and difficult time. You will need a hands-on lawyer as well as someone who will generally hold your hand. Make sure you secure the finest help.

22

NEVER GO INTO COURT WITHOUT FIRST MEETING AND APPROVING OF YOUR ADVOCATE

'He speaks to me as if I was a public meeting.'

QUEEN VICTORIA

*I*F ALL ATTEMPTS at negoti-
ation fail, the disputes outstanding with your spouse will
eventually proceed to court. Facing your spouse before a
judge will be a stressful and also a pivotal experience,
determining as it will issues concerning the future well-being
of your children and your relations with them and/or the
disposition of your income and property.

Familiar with every aspect in dispute, your solicitor will
have worked closely with you. By then you will have estab-
lished a solid professional relationship. Your solicitor will
appreciate the strength of your case and its weaknesses, the
history of your matrimonial affairs, your personality and that
of your spouse. Having conducted settlement talks, there will
also be an understanding of the differences between the two
sides. An awareness of the sticking points in the claims
between you will be a significant factor in deciding on the
best way to present your evidence.

In short, it is to be hoped that by the time you come to
trial you will feel, and be, well prepared. But who is to
present your case? If it is to be someone other than your
solicitor, it makes sense that you should have met with them
earlier, had the opportunity to discuss matters in detail,

including tactics, and satisfied yourself that you have confidence in them to represent you.

This may sound axiomatic but you would be surprised how often in our system people only meet their barrister for the first time outside the door of the court.

Nothing could be more unsettling. In theory, the barrister will have been selected by your solicitor but that is no guarantee that they will have met or worked together before. Often, when a brief is delivered, the barrister appointed to take it is chosen by the clerk in chambers rather than the solicitor and then, sometimes, only the night before!

This should be avoided. Barristers are often accused of being remote or condescending and there is no point in having someone to represent you who may have only just picked up the papers and in whom you have no personal grounds for confidence, whatever their reputed expertise.

Any court hearing, particularly one concerned with the definitive determination of major areas of disagreement, is going to be of immense importance to you. It will be traumatic enough without having to worry about your barrister. Having gone so far, it is only right that you should approve of your advocate. The test is, are you happy for them to represent you?

23

DO NOT GET INVOLVED
WITH YOUR LAWYER
EMOTIONALLY

'Woe unto you, lawyers! for ye have taken away the Key of
Knowledge.'

ST LUKE'S GOSPEL xi.52

*I*N FEW, IF any, chapters of
your life will you have more actual need of the skill, judgement, independence and expertise that are the hallmark of a
true professional.

You will meet your lawyer initially in a state of considerable emotional distress. You will look to them for direction,
guidance, understanding. You will require their help, appreciate their advice, come to rely on them, even depend on
them.

You may even come to enjoy your dealings with them.
They understand your concerns, are sympathetic, sometimes
make you feel better. Fighting your battles for you, they will
be involved with you, achieving results that will affect you
and your family for years to come. But never make the mistake of believing that that involvement is other than a professional one.

A problem shared is a problem halved. You will feel
relieved, grateful, free to contact them when you need to.
The more they achieve for you, the more you will admire
them. The harder the case, the greater the contrast may
appear between them and your spouse. You will make the

comparison, ask about their family, get to know them better, become friends.

During all of this time you will be in a vulnerable state. Vulnerability and gratitude do not mix. Whilst you have need of their help, you should allow nothing to compromise the quality of your lawyer's advice. Keep your relationship strictly on a lawyer-client basis. What happens after your divorce is beyond the scope of this book.

SECTION SIX

❖

CHILDREN'S ISSUES

24

ALWAYS PUT THE BEST INTERESTS OF THE CHILDREN FIRST

'Children begin by loving their parents: after a time they judge them; rarely, if ever, do they forgive them.'

OSCAR WILDE: *A Woman of No Importance*

*H*OW CAN TWO people intent on severing their marital relationship at the same time work together to continue their parenting relationship? How can you dissolve a marriage and preserve a family? Isn't that just a contradiction in terms?

Consider the reality. You and your spouse are divorcing each other, you are not divorcing the children. That is a fact of life. Another is that the children probably love you both. They need you both too, indeed they have a right to you both, with all the responsibility, pleasure, pain and joy which that entails. They are not like matrimonial assets to be divided up or disposed of. They belong to the two of you in equal measure. Nothing can ever change that.

But how do you live with the continuation of the family when all you want is to be divorced from your spouse? How can you be expected to maintain contact with your spouse because of the children? Surely it will involve speaking to each other over any number of matters, seeing each other regularly with contact visits, and then there will be birthdays, school concerts, graduations, even weddings. Won't it go on forever?

Yes, it will and how you handle it will have a powerful impact on the lives of your children.

Remember the two things that we discussed that you must always do:

BE POSITIVE
KEEP MATTERS IN PERSPECTIVE.

In no other context are they more valid or important. Now, duly applying these two, add a third:

ALWAYS PUT THE CHILDREN'S BEST INTERESTS FIRST.

Easily said, maybe, but it is the only way to proceed. If you have any doubts, put yourself in your children's place. It is essential that the children come through the divorce with the least long-term disturbance. If you can recognize this, you are half-way there. You will also see that no-one but you and your spouse can make it happen, that you have to co-operate for the children's sakes.

As husband and wife, the decision to get divorced rests with you. The children have no say in it. As parents, the responsibility for bringing the children through the divorce is yours as well. You have to explain matters to them, establish clear ground rules for when you split up, make sure things work. How they emerge from it is up to you. If you can co-operate with your spouse so that each of you can love and care for your children free of conflict, the children will have the best chance of coming out of it unscathed. Anything less and they run the risk of becoming victims of the divorce, just as you were the victim of your marriage, but without the security, maturity or support to be able to cope.

Think positively. It is obviously best for the children to maintain the family relationships that were part of their lives before the divorce and quite clearly they will be better off when their parents are supportive and co-operative, than when they are not. It is far better, also, for children to be told the truth. Not only will this enable them to know where they stand but, just as importantly, it will maintain their trust in you.

Keep matters in perspective. They are your children. Your duty to protect them as best you can is not dissolved with your marriage. It will survive until the children are grown up, maybe forever: so will the unique jointness of your parenthood.

Remember this: be prepared to put the best interests of the children first, and you should have no lasting problems. Indeed, you may feel that you have managed to salvage something that is of great value and was never fully appreciated before.

Of course, it is not easy. Children and how to cope with them are difficult enough in marriage. They must be the most problematic aspect of any divorce, easily the most painful. Thinking positively, this is all the more reason for you to consider how to deal with it at the outset and make sure you get it right. Run the whole divorce through in your mind from the children's point of view and adjust your course accordingly. If something is not in their best interests, then change it. Consider their feelings as well as their welfare. They are every bit as human as you and a lot more vulnerable. So have courage. Protect them from the fall-out of your divorce as best you can. Doing the right thing cannot be that difficult. Your children love both of you. That love is ever hopeful.

25

TRY NOT TO INVOLVE THE
CHILDREN IN CONTROVERSY

*'The fathers have eaten sour grapes, and the children's teeth are
set on edge.'*

EZEKIEL XVIII.2

WHEN THINGS ARE bad and
getting worse in a marriage, everything becomes an argument, nothing is agreed. People fight about anything, they
even fight over what constitutes the best interests of the
children.

The simple, obvious rule is to try not to involve the children in the break-up of your marital relationship. As things
deteriorate, do not row in front of them or at least not so
they can hear. Imagine what it must be like for a small child,
lying awake in bed, listening to their parents abusing and
tearing into each other. How much worse if they are then
brought into the process with Mummy criticizing Daddy,
Daddy accusing Mummy, each parent pressuring the child
to take sides.

Try to understand your children. At the best of times,
children want a good relationship with both parents. How
much more is that the case in time of divorce? Despite
divorce, each one of you remains a parent to your children.
You may well have come to loathe the sight of each other
but your children are very unlikely to feel the same way
about either of you. Never forget children need both parents.
You must be sensitive to that. Do your best not to impose
your own attitudes, so that your children may love both

parents without guilt. As you have a right to your feelings, they have an identical right to theirs, so do not erect barriers to prevent them from seeing and speaking to your ex-spouse. Recognize their feelings. Seek to correct the hurt of the past by behaving responsibly towards them in the future.

You and your ex-spouse jointly remain the most important influences in your children's lives. You are still their role models, so do your best together to adjust constructively to the changes wrought by the divorce. Try to understand what your children are thinking; try not to speak ill of each other or talk of broken homes. All children have a fundamental need for security. Promise yourselves, therefore, that you will each do your best to fulfil that need. Be positive about your new lives and the altered relationships with your children. With fear and disagreements kept to yourselves, the least harm will be done to them.

People often say, in the context of divorce, that children are resilient, that they will manage to cope with the breakdown of their parents' marriage. Many do. Yet, so many do not and even more who appear to do so take their scars with them through life.

Divorce is an emotional uprooting for a child. It takes sensitivity and skill to avoid causing them lasting damage. The children who get through unharmed are those whose parents have managed their disagreements so as to avoid involving the children. In this way the children are not forced to choose between their parents, they are not involved in critical discussions or decisions. They are left to be children with the same family ties and united support from their parents.

The importance of being conscious of the pitfalls for your children, of planning for this aspect carefully, cannot be overstated. The difference between getting it right and getting it wrong can be devastating. A child's future happiness and emotional stability are at stake, factors which will follow them through life. Guilt, depression, delinquency are often the results of parents getting it wrong.

When you think of how difficult it is at the best of times to bring a child up properly within a marriage, you will see the odds shorten against you on divorce. All the more reason for a concerted, joint effort on this aspect in full co-operation with your spouse. The children are the innocent parties. It abuses them if that is ever forgotten.

26

TRY NOT TO LOSE CONTACT WITH YOUR CHILDREN

'In war, whichever side may call itself the victor,
there are no winners, but all are losers.'

NEVILLE CHAMBERLAIN, 1938

A BY-PRODUCT INCREAS-
INGLY of divorce, already observed and documented, is the
growth of the extended family, where new relationships are
created by divorce and re-marriage, endowing people with a
feeling of kinship that often embraces several families at any
one time.

Originating with step-families the phenomenon can go
further stretching, for example, from the child of your ex-
husband's new wife to the child through re-marriage of your
new husband's ex-wife. Although not related in any way the
two children can, and often will, grow up with a feeling of
kinship, as part of an extended step-family.

Looking at the harm that can be caused to children
as a result of divorce, it is a welcome but, it is to be
hoped, not a pious thought that rather than be broken up
by the parents divorcing, a family unit may instead find
itself enlarged to provide an increased level of love and
support for its children. With one divorce for every two
marriages in the United Kingdom, and over one third
of all marriages being re-marriages when one or both
of the couples have been divorced, this trend is likely to
continue.

But what of the children who, following on divorce each

year, lose contact with one of their parents? The parent disappears. The children do not know where they are. They neither see them nor hear from them again – no birthday card, no phone call, no communication of any kind. No support from a new extended family will ever quite make up for their loss. It is as if that parent had ceased to exist, certainly ceased to care.

These children are the real victims of divorce, the refugees from parental disputes. There are tens of thousands of them, for each year up to 40,000 fathers alone choose not to contact their children! Why? Because the father cannot bear to see the mother? Because the children have moved with their mother, too far away for their father to see them conveniently? Because the mother has brain-washed the children against him? Because there was too much unpleasantness when the father did see them? Because the father cannot bear the idea of his children living with their mother's new man? Because the father owes the mother money for the children's support which he cannot afford to pay? Because the father has started a new family and his new partner does not want him to have anything to do with his old family?

We have already said it is the parents who do the divorcing, not the children. A father will remain the father till the end of time. So why, even, as sometimes happens, when the children say they no longer wish to see the father, does a father abandon his children? Is it because of any of the reasons above?

Who knows? Yet maybe there is an additional, altogether more poignant reason. In contrast to the other instances all of which depend on outside influence, this reason arises from a father's innermost feelings about himself. Some fathers convince themselves that they have been thoroughly bad parents. Looking back, they realize that they never appreciated their time with their children. Away far more frequently than with them when they were together, paying the children little or no attention, never getting to know them, regarding them at best as a noisy nuisance. With the children now living with their mother, the father suddenly sees what he has lost. He is overwhelmed. Never having created proper bonds, he feels himself an outsider, a failure in parenting terms.

Some fathers in this position write off their relationship with their children. They believe that the children have no love for them, want nothing to do with them. Filled with remorse, they believe it is all too late.

These fathers are as tragic and ill-advised as all the others who have deliberately lost contact with their children. It is all such a waste. Although it may take a lot of hard work and dedicated effort, a father-child relationship may actually deepen and develop after a divorce. It may not be easy, but, as with everything in life, the more you put into it, the more you will get out.

From the children's point of view it must be bewildering never to hear from their father again. Their relationship with their father is unique. The same flesh and blood, their father is not just some other man. Their own physical, mental and emotional make-up is partly determined by his genes. Who can say what harm will be caused if contact is lost? The emotional damage in later years can be immense.

There can only be losers when a parent gives up contact, whether it is the father or, in fewer cases, the mother. No-one can define what might have happened if contact had been maintained. No-one can say whether it would have been good or bad. What we can say, however, is that without it, there must always be a gaping hole in the lives of the children and of the missing parent as well, the effect of which is incalculable.

However impossible the situation may appear, think long and hard before breaking off contact.

27

DO NOT OVERLOOK GRANDPARENTS

'Two grandmothers meet each other, proudly wheeling new
grandchildren in prams.
"What a lovely grandchild, Mrs Goldberg. Such a beautiful baby!"
"Thank you, Mrs Finestein. But wait till you see the photographs!"'

JOKE

GRANDPARENTS CAN BE useful. Their relationship with your children can impart a sense of roots, of belonging, of continuity, of family history, qualities that will add a dimension to a child's self-awareness and perspective on life. Grandparents can be a source of great affection too, forming the most important of bonds with your children outside of your own, providing them with added stability and security. They love their grandchildren regardless of what has happened to the parents.

They may be convenient as well. It is said that by enjoying their grandchildren and then returning them to the parents, grandparents have all the fun with none of the responsibility, but they have their uses: for baby-sitting, helping with the costs of maintaining and educating the children, taking the children on outings and treats, having them to stay so you can get away.

As children grow up, they develop their own relationship with their grandparents. This is often very close. As they get older, children often find that they can talk more easily with grandparents than parents. They trust them. Grandparents can become a bridge to the parents, a support when needed, a source of strength, all the things that you might have need of in a divorce.

Do not dismiss this when times get rough. Grandparents, from either side of the family, may be just what is needed to provide extra comfort and confidence to the children and help them adjust. They may facilitate contact when this is most needed and difficult to achieve; they may step in as surrogate parents, when times are rough.

If they did not exist, they would have to be invented. Indeed, the law recognizes their unique position by affording them rights to contact and, in exceptional circumstances, rights to apply for a residence order.

Grandparents are not a new creation. As the most visible part of the extended family, they have always had a signific-ant role to play in family life, often standing in for parents when parents were at work, thereby averting or reducing the strains and tensions that lead to divorce.

It is no coincidence therefore, that as extended families have declined, the divorce rate has shot up. It is never too late to rediscover them, nor indeed, the web of uncles, aunts and cousins who together make up the extended family, all of whom can still play their part in providing support to parents and children alike.

It would be ironic if it is divorce that brings us back to the extended family again; but, blood is thicker than water and there is no more solid help available to a child whose parents split up, than family help from grandparents down.

SECTION SEVEN

❖

LAW AND PROCEDURE

28

BLAME IS OUT,
RESPONSIBILITY IN

'Then farewell, Horace; whom I hated so,
Not for thy faults, but mine.'

BYRON: *Childe Harold* iv

SEPARATE ANY TWO children having a fight and each one will tell you that the other caused it and is to blame. Blaming somebody else goes back to the Garden of Eden. It is an integral part of human nature. For the person doing the blaming it serves to legitimize and justify their actions, however out of proportion or bloody these may be. That is how children behave. They point a finger and shout.

So do we.

When it comes to divorce, the notion of having someone to blame is embedded deep within our collective psyche. Until the reforms come into effect the law will still reflect this view. For the old law will continue for some while, possibly until the beginning of 1999, and under the old law fault is a means to divorce.

For many people the breaking of marriage vows is not just regrettable, it is inherently wrong. They believe that the party breaking their vows should pay a price. Marital failure implies wrong doing. It follows that one of the parties is guilty.

But guilty of what?

How often have we heard people say:

'Everything was absolutely fine, until . . .'

'It would never have happened if . . .'

'I only did it, because . . .'

These are all normal responses to the reality of marital breakdown. The speakers place themselves in the role of victim, having had neither control over events, nor responsibility for what has happened.

It is this attitude, exactly, that the old divorce law formalized, when, by providing for quickie divorces on the grounds of unreasonable behaviour, adultery or desertion, it added a layer of statutory blame to the miseries of the respondent. The law blamed the respondent for the marriage breakdown, exonerating the petitioner from all responsibility for its collapse, even though, all too often, the allegations of fault were a complete fiction.

It is possible to proceed in this way, if both parties agree, but if they do not, then the procedure is bound to lead to problems; and yet, fast, avoiding a delay of at least two years for a divorce by consent, and unlikely to be defended, many petitioners embrace it without due thought or understanding. In this way three quarters of all divorces are brought into the realms of conflict.

Research shows that it is conflict between parents which has been linked to greater social and behavioural problems among children, rather than the divorce itself. The result, in far too many families, is that the love and respect between the parents and children have become the prime casualties of the divorce.

Once the Family Law Act 1996 comes into force everything will be reversed. People will no longer be thrown into contention; fault-based divorce will be abolished; responsibility for what has happened to their marriage and for the consequences of breaking it will rest with the parties themselves.

In other words, blame, which used to be heaped on the respondent, will be out, and responsibility, previously abjured by the petitioner, will be in.

No wonder that the new legislation excited such fierce and wide-ranging opposition. It has caused a revolution. For not only will the Act change the law, as explained briefly in Appendix IV, but in doing so it will also change the assumptions on which the law is based.

Having banished fault as a means to divorce, it will be necessary to complete the revolution by bringing the hearts and minds of those involved in divorce and marital breakdown into line with the new law.

For, under the new system, one party will no longer blame the other and disown responsibility. When pursuing a divorce reality will have to be faced, a reality that was ignored by the old law. Nothing but good can come from blame being out and responsibility in, for in wisdom this is how the law should have always recognized life to be.

There can be any number of reasons for marriages irretrievably breaking down. Many may involve fault, but there will be an equal, or even greater number where blame neither need nor should be attached. In many instances the parties have grown apart. Things have changed between them, they wish to go their separate ways. Each of them accepts a measure of responsibility for the breakdown. They would prefer to have a civilized divorce without recrimination, for what is the good of apportioning blame, especially if only the grossest examples of unreasonable behaviour bear on the children and finances? But no. The old law says you can proceed without contention, only if you are prepared to wait for a period of two years' separation. If you want a divorce sooner, one of you must first adduce evidence that the other has behaved unreasonably. Only then, when somebody has been found to have been in the wrong, will the court grant a divorce.

One would have thought that divorce was traumatic enough without the system conspiring to put people in contention. In the real world, married couples can be unhappy when neither of them behaves unreasonably.

When marriages go wrong, more often than not, it is because husbands and wives develop separately and grow apart. It is not because either party is wholly to blame. Using the language of the old law, in truth, marriages rarely break down as a result of unreasonable behaviour. They break down because no-one dealt with the problems that led to the behaviour in the first place. Nine times out of ten, the unreasonable behaviour complained of, and, it has to be said, also the adultery or desertion, are the *symptoms* of what went wrong with the marriage. They are not the actual cause of the breakdown.

To test this, let us consider a typical 'unreasonable behaviour' petition, such as might be drafted under the old system. Amongst other things one might plead that the wife likes to read in the evening and listen to classical music, whilst the husband *insists* on watching television. It is the *insistence* that makes the behaviour unreasonable. If it had been the husband's petition he would have said that the insistence was the wife's. Yet did it really prove that one party was at fault and therefore to blame for the marriage breakdown? If so, which? And why? Surely, if anything, the behaviour shows that the couple has grown apart. Both share a mutual responsibility for that. Should that not have been enough, without apportioning blame?

We all recognize that a joint effort is required to make a marriage work. People often do not realize that the same applies if a marriage is not to fail.

If, as should be its function, the law prefers to preserve marriages, then it should be concerned with trying to save them. What caused the parties to grow apart? Did they try to discuss their difficulties or seek outside help? Under the new system, the minimum period of twelve or eighteen months, between the initial information meeting and the granting of the divorce, is intended to provide couples with an opportunity to do this.

The couple will know that they have acted responsibly, for responsibility should and will be an absolute essential to bringing a marriage to an end. Each party will have their own measure of responsibility for the marriage breakdown. As we have seen, the acceptance of that responsibility is a major part of the healing process. So is forgiveness and the ability to feel comfortable with oneself, but, almost perversely, all were negated by the old law.

Like St Augustine's famous prayer for chastity, the reforms are not to take effect 'just yet'. But whatever the delay, the old law stands discredited, as will be obvious when there is a rush to obtain quickie divorces before the new law finally comes into effect.

Try to resist that rush. Try to change your perspective with the new law. For no good ever came from dwelling on blame. No point was ever served in rehearsing the mistakes of a marriage in divorce proceedings.

However hurt and upset you may feel, do try to understand that.

The old law is coming to an end. No longer need there be any bar to a positive approach to divorce. It is time to dust yourself down, to move on, to select your goal and keep to it. Divorce is a rebirth, if only people would see it that way. Only then will feelings be spared and suffering reduced.

When you point a finger at someone, three fingers are

pointing back at you. It might not always be easy to accept your share of responsibility, dismissing all thoughts of fault and blame, but always remember those three fingers. It is time to be honest with yourself, above all to be positive.

29
ALWAYS PLAY BY THE RULES

'I had an aunt in Yucatan
Who bought a Python from a man
And kept it for a pet.
She died, because she never knew
Those simple little rules and few:–
The Snake is living yet.'

HILAIRE BELLOC: *More Beasts for Worse Children*

*T*HE LAW IS immutable. It is therefore appropriate that we should always play by its rules. The law is far-reaching. If we break it, we should not be surprised if it rises up and hits us like a garden rake.

When I was a young articled clerk, I was in a restaurant one evening when I noticed a man with a pretty girl at the next table. I recognized him as the husband of a client, who was in the process of divorcing him. I knew this from a photograph she had given me so that a private detective could obtain evidence of his adultery. Unfortunately, the detective spent three nights watching the wrong apartment. But that night, fate yielded us the husband. For as well as adultery, the finances were in issue. He was with his mistress. He left with her after settling his bill with a very large roll of banknotes!

We are all entitled to a lucky break sometimes. The husband, in that case, was caught out. When you are caught out, no-one believes you about anything. It can prove very expensive.

In another much later case, this happened on a large scale.

I was again acting for the wife, whose husband talked at her. He never stopped talking at her and never listened to what she had to say. Her life was miserable but, before she began her divorce, she turned things to her advantage.

The husband's finances were substantial and also very complex. So, one evening, she asked him to explain them to her. This he did, talking at her for almost an hour. What he didn't know was that his wife had recorded everything that he had said, using a video camera hidden behind the curtains.

When the divorce began, we knew that the husband's solicitors had made only partial disclosures of his means. It was not their fault, they repeated what he had told them. When they were told about the tape, they asked to hear it. We declined, saying they could hear it only if we decided to use it. The husband was thrown into great confusion. He could not remember what he had told his wife, so he settled handsomely.

There are many more stories that would persuade anyone to abide by the rules. To show the kind of passions that finances engender, I had another case acting for a husband, whose wife refused to believe that he had no more assets hidden away. After the case was resolved in court, the wife made an anonymous call to the Inland Revenue. A lengthy and expensive investigation ensued from which the husband emerged unscathed, though several thousands of pounds poorer for his accountant's costs.

The world of matrimonial finances could be straight out of Roald Dahl. Imagine a jungle crossed by a network of paths, some marked *passions*, some marked *rules*. If they can, the passions will lunge at you and gobble you up, so it is essential that you avoid them and stick to the rules. You must not deviate, dally, or try to take a short cut. You must not hurry, seem frightened, or try to give up. Most people need an expert guide to get through. It is cheaper to accept an expert than to get it wrong.

Everything has to be disclosed. Everything. Statements for bank accounts, credit cards, mortgages, brokers, stores, expenses, petrol; cheque stubs, tax returns, bills, receipts, school fee plans, investments, school fees, pensions, health insurance, valuations, general insurances; the cost of food, house-keeping, family, cars, holidays, clothes, house maintenance, travel, entertainment.

Every item will be seized upon and scrutinized. A credit card statement, a cheque stub. What were you doing in that restaurant? Who were you with? How did you pay for it? Where is the bill? Questions will inundate you like tropical rain. You must not be afraid. Keep calm, keep going. Don't look back. You'll get through in the end, but only because you stuck to the right path!

30

NEVER ABUSE PROCEDURES; NEVER FAIL TO TAKE PROTECTIVE STEPS; NEVER ALLOW YOUR SPOUSE TO AVOID THE RULES

'Ignorance of the law excuses no man:
not that all men know the law, but because 'tis an excuse every man
will plead, and no man can tell how to confute him.'

JOHN SELDEN: *Table Talk*

As WITH SO much in life, the effective conduct of matrimonial proceedings boils down to strategy. Select the right route, exercise the right balance, do not get lost. We will see in the next section on costs that every letter that your solicitor writes or receives, every telephone call, every application he makes on your behalf, will cost money. Even if you succeed at the end of the day, the costs will come out of a finite family purse, leaving less available for other things. As always, or at least as it is always said, in litigation the lawyers are the only real winners.

All the more reason to maintain a proper sense of proportion. You can do the most terrible things to your spouse in matrimonial proceedings, your spouse can do the most terrible things to you. But this is not warfare. Even though you have access to a nuclear arsenal there will be no need to use nuclear weapons. In nearly every case, rapiers will be sufficient, although you may find that the occasional mortar shell will be helpful to get people going. On a financial level, the matrimonial process is merely a legal procedure used to disentangle the threads of two lives. It involves unravelling the threads where they have become intertwined, straightening them, counting them and finally deciding how many should be awarded to each party to enable them to begin a fresh life.

An obvious and sensible process, it can nevertheless be used to cause the greatest discomfort and embarrassment to an unlucky spouse. Depending on the circumstances a host of orders may be applied for. These range from freezing orders to enforcement orders, ejection orders, punitive orders, restraining orders, orders for sale, unless orders, lump sum orders, maintenance orders, transfer orders, attachment orders, interim orders, orders for costs. There are others too. Enough for one party to make the other squirm. Enough to lead to injustice.

Other initiatives are properly available also, as an everyday part of the process. Interrogatories, questionnaires, affidavits, cross-petitions, replies, Calderbank offers . . . the list goes on. All are perfectly respectable but all can be used to excess, to harass a party. They should be employed with proper restraint.

Matrimonial proceedings should be conducted amicably. There is no need, particularly between lawyers, why they should not be. If this is not possible, they should be pursued fairly. That is not to say that protective steps, such as registering a charge to protect your right to live in the matrimonial home, should not be taken to safeguard your interests. They should. You should never fail to take such steps and should never allow anyone to advise you otherwise. You should also ensure that your spouse complies with the rules so that matters may be resolved fairly.

But keeping an eye to the future, what you do today will affect your tomorrow. All litigation is miserable. It is draining, too. You will have to live with yourself. You will want to feel comfortable. There is no point in mortgaging your health or your emotions for the sake of greed, spite or revenge. Your lawyer should be a warrior, not an assassin. Seek a just result and be happy with it!

SECTION EIGHT

❖

COSTS

31

TRY NOT TO
WASTE COSTS

'A man who knows the price of everything and the value of nothing.'
OSCAR WILDE: *Lady Windermere's Fan*

WHEN PEOPLE REPLY to a question with a question, you can be sure they do not know the answer.

'How long is a piece of string?' is a fine example. It is the standard answer to the question: 'How much is this going to cost me?' Like Cold War spies identifying themselves on a park bench in a coded exchange: 'The crocuses are early in Prague this year' – 'I always buy my shoes in Santiago', you know that you and your solicitor have made contact. You also know that you will never get a better response.

There is a reason for this. You may not believe it, but your solicitor really does not know. Why not? I am tempted to respond, 'Why should he?' but I won't. The reason is, it depends on how the proceedings develop. Solicitors will give you their charging rates, they will let you have estimates for specific items like an undefended divorce, with agreement on the children, and one day in court on the finances; but even they will hedge their figures to prepare for trial or, before that, to extract information from the other side.

The key word is time. Solicitors live by time, charging you for it as if they would have been better employed on something else had it not been for your matter. It would be as well to check with them to see what sort of things get charged for.

The answer might surprise you but do understand that letters going out have to be dictated, letters coming in will have to be read, and time will be spent travelling to meetings on your behalf. There will be telephone conversations and correspondence you know nothing about; barristers and other experts will have to be instructed, time will be spent on drafting, assistants will be engaged to look after the papers and do research; even pleasantries on the telephone will find their way onto the time sheet. Disbursements will mount up too, for photocopying, faxes, couriers, taxis, even lunches with you, if devoted to your case. It all adds up.

Most solicitors will be aware of this and keep you advised of how much is being incurred. However, it is only common sense to keep on top of your costs. You are not signing a blank cheque and should not be made to feel that you are. It is you who retains the solicitor, not the other way round.

If you are not happy with how your solicitor is handling your case or dealing with the costs, do not throw good money away, move to another solicitor. Ask to have regular accounts, perhaps on a monthly basis, in a form that sets out in detail what you have been charged and the cost of each service. If any items do not seem reasonable to you, then say so. Use your solicitor's time sensibly. Remember that time costs money. Make the best use of that time to ensure that you receive maximum value. Restrict yourself to legal questions: whenever possible, save up your questions for a single conversation or meeting.

There is a problem, however, that concerns the costs that your spouse is incurring on the other side. Think of dance steps – their costs will broadly mirror your own. As I explain below, these all come out of the same pot. You may find that the piece of string has become a rope. If you are unlucky, you may wish to use it on your lawyer. But, again, if only matters can be pursued sensibly, this sort of situation should not arise.

For if things really can be agreed sensibly at the outset, quite possibly at an early meeting with your spouse and yourself and your respective solicitors, then it is quite possible to set a budget and many thousands of pounds may be saved. It all comes back to positive thinking, setting a goal and resolving to come through the divorce in good shape. At the very least, an initial meeting will highlight the differences between you. Consider these calmly and you may be surprised at how much is agreed. If not, you can take a view with your solicitors on the options available to you, always bearing in mind the merits and relative importance of the matters outstanding, and the likely cost of fighting. You may have no alternative other than to fight but, if you do, keep the costs under review and remember that there is seldom a case which, at some stage, it will not be possible to settle.

The simple rule is, do not waste costs.

32

DO NOT FORGET
THAT COSTS COME OUT OF A
SINGLE FAMILY POT

'As the crackling of thorns under a pot, so is the laughter of a fool.'
ECCLESIASTES i.6

I REMEMBER ONCE SEEING a letter before action, which had been addressed to a husband only to be returned to the solicitor friend of mine who had sent it, with a message scrawled diagonally across it: 'As I will be paying your costs, permit me one comment: *****!' That husband realized something that a surprising number of parties to a divorce only perceive when it is too late. There is only a finite amount of money to be divided between the family and the costs have to be met from the same fund.

It is only after the fighting is over that a tally can be made. It can then come as a real shock when it is seen that the thousands spent by both sides on their lawyers come to more than the total difference between the parties when they were at their most implacable! After so much stress and strain, it is the last straw. Both sides end up hating each other and their lawyers. With all the fight drained from them by the proceedings, they feel disappointed and let down. It is then, when they have lost their passion, that they can see how wise it would have been to have adopted a more pragmatic and positive approach at the beginning.

I cannot emphasize enough how sensible and, with hindsight, how obvious it is to cut the emotion from your calculations in pursuing your divorce. If your solicitor can help you to do this, they will have more than earned their fees. Just as with your emotional capital, so it is important to preserve the family capital for use during divorce. You would never dream of drawing a blank cheque against it in any other circumstance. Why do it now?

SECTION NINE

❖

RECONCILIATION AND MEDIATION

33

NEVER SAY NEVER

'If, of all words of tongue and pen
The saddest are, "It might have been"
More sad are those we daily see
"It is, but hadn't ought to be!"'

BRET HARTE: *Mrs Judge Jenkins*

A SOLICITOR SHOULD never institute divorce proceedings for a client without making sure that they really do understand what they are doing, and that there is no chance of a reconciliation. The curious thing is that the clients are often too close to their own problems to appreciate that things could be other than as they see them. We can all recognize the problems in others but seldom can we see them in ourselves.

Saying that you want a divorce may really mean something else: an acknowledgement, certainly, that things are bad and cannot continue. It may mean instead that you want your marriage to improve, that you need to make positive changes to ensure that it does. You did not marry to get divorced. 'I want a divorce' is often the shock that leads to improvement. Marriages need constant working at to succeed. Most people do work hard to have good marriages but they do not work as hard as a divorced person at putting their lives back together. With motivation and common cause it requires far less effort and energy to work at improving your marriage, than getting over it once it has failed.

We have already talked about growing apart. It is shorthand for saying: 'We still love each other. We just can't stand living together any more.' A familiar refrain? Although each case is different, maybe it really means that the old ways of relating to each other no longer work. Can the marriage be saved? Should you want it to be? If there is still love and respect between you, a genuine sense of mutual forgiveness, a sharing of responsibility for each party's hurt and unhappiness, a desire to move from old, destructive ways, and a will to recreate a new relationship within the marriage, then yes it can, and it should be saved.

Why it has gone wrong and how to save it is best left to expert, outside help. Nature has a way of protecting us from emotional pain. We go numb, so it is not always easy for people to understand, themselves, why they have grown apart. What started as a small but real resentment (something your spouse might never have been aware of) can fester and grow out of all proportion, eating away like a cancer until the marriage is dead.

I once had a client who, having kept some grievance to herself for seven years, erupted at her husband. He swore he had no idea what his wife was so upset about, but she had bottled it up for so long, that when she finally exploded it was too late. The marriage was over. Had she been able to discuss the problem earlier, who knows how things might have transpired?

The key to any reconciliation is to dig deeper and deeper until you unearth whatever it was that caused things to go wrong in the first place. The chances are that neither of you will have been aware of its impact. Its discovery may even come as a surprise to the party who was hurt by it initially. It may have been forgotten as it lay buried under level upon level of additional resentment and hurt. For one thing is sure, whoever sustained the first cut will have struck back at the other, if not directly, then by some change in attitude or demeanour. It is all a question of reaction. A web of disappointment and misery will exist, to be unravelled or left untouched.

I mention this towards the end of this book as many people, when they first see a solicitor, are unsure of whether they really want a divorce. Those of you in that position who have read this far may still wish to give some thought to reconciliation. Having discussed the practical considerations of divorcing, you will now have a better idea, if not exactly of what is involved in divorce, at least of what you should aim for and the pitfalls you should avoid.

Some useful addresses appear in Appendix I, which may provide you with the kind of help you will need. As a preliminary you could do worse than this:

1. Remember when you were happy in your marriage, then dig into your memory to see if you can isolate any single matter, however long ago, which may have caused things initially to go wrong;

2. If you can, then try to cut the impact of that matter out of your feelings, as if it had been forgiven or had never happened;

3. Looking back in that way, do things appear different? If they do, then does that matter in retrospect still seem important?

If you have been able to go back far enough, you will have distinguished symptoms from causes (i.e. if there has been adultery, you will have gone back further to see what may have brought it about) and gained a considerable insight into your problems. If you cannot discuss them with your spouse, then go and talk to a friend, your GP, or someone on the list in Appendix I. You never know, with a lot of hard work, it may be possible, even now, to get your marriage back on the tracks.

34
MAYBE

'. . . patience and goodwill will in the end conciliate the goodwill
of others.'

EMPRESS JOSEPHINE: Letter to her children

*I*F RECONCILIATION IS suc-
cessful, there is no more to be done, save, most importantly,
to see that henceforth every effort is made to ensure that the
marriage works. Every relationship needs working at. Every
successful relationship is worked at all the time.

But what if, as happens quite often, and without reflecting
on the parties in any way, attempts at reconciliation come
to nothing? Then the concept of conciliation may be just
what is needed.

What is it? A civilized way of resolving disputes arising
on a divorce or separation. At worst, it does not work and
no harm is done. At best, it achieves a reconciliation between
the parties, in all but emotional terms; in other words, a
method of resolving all matters in issue, except for the continuation of the marriage, in harmony, with fairness and
without rancour. It can be a triumph of sound common sense.

Conciliation and reconciliation have come to us straight
from the Latin (conciliare and reconciliare). The Romans
stopped at nothing to achieve their ends, conquering most
of the world as they knew it in the process. And yet, their
power having been won through force of arms, they also
perfected the art of conciliation, of making peace between
two parties, as an alternative to combat. For often, it is the

knowledge of the perils of conflict that persuade people that conflict is best avoided.

We do not need to think of the wars going on around us today, to see that this is still true. We need look no further than our own court system. It is an adversarial system in which one party wins and the other loses. In divorce terms, to win the contest in court, members of the same family become antagonists, their children caught up in the cross-fire between them.

It is an expensive, bloody, unpleasant business, substantially adding to the distress already suffered by an increasing proportion of society with the rise in the rate of divorce.

How inspired, therefore, for a system to emerge in which there are no losers? How obvious for parties to be encouraged to negotiate on a friendly basis and come up with solutions that everyone – husband, wife and children – can live with?

Both inspired and obvious, there is such a system. It is used by an increasing number of people every year.

Perhaps the word conciliation is too reminiscent of labour disputes for it to remain apt today for matrimonial matters. In any event, mediation is the word used to describe this alternative process to court proceedings, which, if successful, saves emotions, time and money.

It is a process in which an impartial third person, the mediator, assists those involved in family breakdowns to reach their own agreed joint decisions on matters inevitably arising on separation or divorce – the separation or divorce itself, arrangements for the children and all questions of finance and property.

Mediation is a voluntary process, it cannot be imposed. Therefore agreement arising as a result of it can only be reached with the acquiescence of both parties.

Of course, mediation will not work for everyone, but

featuring prominently in the Lord Chancellor's Reforms and in use in many other jurisdictions around the world, it is clearly something which is going to remain with us and develop. Indeed, it will probably grow in its appeal, in due course becoming the preferred procedure for resolving matrimonial disputes.

A more detailed and practical explanation of what mediation means is included in Appendix III. Prepared by National Family Mediation, you will see that the aims of mediation are entirely consistent with the Reach Target. If mediation can enable you to avoid conflict, achieve a fair settlement and get on with your life with relationships intact, there is much to be said for it.

SECTION TEN

❖

THE FUTURE

35

TRY NOT TO LOOK BACK

'This is not the end. It is not even the beginning of the end.
But it is, perhaps, the end of the beginning.'

WINSTON CHURCHILL, 1942

*T*HERE ARE MANY stages in divorce. Divorce does not begin when you first consult your lawyer. Divorce proceedings are only the end product of a process that has been taking place and developing within you for a considerable while, often for years, before you first take legal advice. The feelings engendered by the disintegration of a marriage are in themselves a kind of emotional divorce. If they counted as divorces themselves, the statistics for failed marriages would easily double.

Every stage in the divorce process, from these initial feelings to the unexpected terror of separation, to the sense of grief as the marriage is mourned, to those very emotions and reactions as set out in Appendix V, will affect, and sometimes overwhelm, most divorcing parties in varying degrees.

This is the divorce process. It does not cease with the Decree Absolute any more than it begins with the filing of the papers. It starts in the heart with the emotional parting, moving on to the head as the process gets under way, remaining there until one distant day when you will realize it has gone.

It all boils down to you. Who are you? That's a good question. After a divorce, you are no longer who you were before you got married. You are single and yet you still feel married. Living alone, you realize the extent that marriage has defined your personal identity. Your former life has gone but your emotional connection with it has not ended. It has shaped your personality to such an extent that you have doubts about your ability to survive on your own as a single person, instead of as part of a couple.

If you do not know who you are, how can anyone else? Divorce can be tremendously destabilizing. For some people, it takes years before they stop feeling married. As with all deep emotions, you will need time to let your feelings settle down.

But that is not all. We have already observed that no-one works harder at putting the pieces of their life back together again than a divorced person. Well, now is the time. It is imperative. Life has marched on. You have to catch up.

Despite all its misery and hurt, divorce is ultimately a process of self-renewal. All birth involves pain, so does rebirth, but being born again you start with the maturity of your experience and the will to prove to yourself that as a single person you are of value and worth in your own right.

You are running to catch up with life now, no longer running away from it. Learn to live on your own, to take care of yourself; do your own shopping, cooking and chores; reach out to your colleagues and friends; be responsible for shaping the direction of your new life; feel accountable to yourself; build up your new identity; let go of the past.

You have set yourself a challenge. The best is ahead of you, not buried in the past. There is nothing to fear from your freedom. One day you will wonder why you ever thought it was impossible to be happy on your own. When you do, you will know who you are. You'll have caught up with life.

36

DO NOT GET
RE-MARRIED ON THE REBOUND

> 'Falling in love again,
> Never wanted to.
> What am I to do?
> Can't help it.'
>
> LERNER

AFTER THEIR DIVORCE, practically all of my female clients of a certain age would tell me that they would never get married again. They meant it, they had been hurt but I had to smile as I told them that, from my experience of other clients, they would find themselves re-married within two to three years. Each one of them shook their heads and laughed but, I believe, each one fulfilled my prediction.

The ancient triumph of hope over experience? Springtime gone mad? As Mrs Thatcher wistfully observed: 'It's a funny old world'? Not at all.

We have already noted that, with a falling marriage rate, one third of all marriages are repeat experiences where one or both of the couple are re-marrying after divorce. That is well over one hundred thousand marriages each year. As some of those marriages will involve couples where both have been married before, it is fair to say that each year a total number of people equal to one half of the number of those divorcing that year, are re-marrying after having themselves been divorced.

And, like my clients, practically every one of them will

have said, at the beginning of their divorce, that they would never marry again! Why? Were they deceiving themselves? Not in any way. For they were sincere when they said they would never marry again, and they were right later when they chose to do so.

All that these apparently contradictory positions indicate is that these persons were not personally ready to enter into another relationship, when they said they would never love one special person again. Later, they have done so because they feel ready to engage in such a relationship, out of a strong belief that the mistakes of the first marriages will not repeat themselves.

Just as significantly, they have discovered during the time that they were single that they wanted another intimate relationship. Human beings need one another. They need to love and be loved. They have found that sharing life with another person is the best kind of life. Feeling renewed as single people, they have felt able to choose partners again.

As well as for having children, the Old Testament views the purpose of marriage as company. Nothing much has changed, even today. People need people.

The only thing to add, without for one moment wishing to spoil the fun, is one word of warning. After a divorce, when people can feel hurt, rejected, unloved, the most natural reaction in the world can be to rush into another relationship to wash away the pain and insecurity. Well and good, if nobody gets hurt, but to jump into another marriage before you have had time to find yourself again, may be an act of great folly.

Give yourself that time. Make sure you know your feelings and have learned the lessons of your divorce and then, and only then, consider re-marriage. There is no time limit. Everyone is unique. Everyone is special, that is why you must be comfortable with your feelings and understand them, to avoid another mistake.

One final thing: as I mention below, on re-marriage, people quite often marry the same kind of person as their first spouse. Think about it!

37

NEVER AGAIN

'It's that man again!'
TED KAVANAGH: BBC *ITMA* programme

*H*UMAN NATURE BEING
what it is, when they told me they would never re-marry, were my female clients (curiously, nearly all of them aged thirty-eight) really seeking re-assurance? Was a part of them wanting me to contradict them, to assure them they were still attractive and suitable for marriage? The need at that time for assurance is quite understandable. The ultimate desire to find another partner and settle down again, even if dressed up as a denial, is more than understandable.

For, eventually, when the battles are lost or won, all of us are human. Suffering during a first marriage, however grave, rarely inhibits people from marrying again. That is how it ought to be. But when they do, there is an overwhelming possibility that they will marry the same kind of person as they did the first time round. Implausible? Maybe, but true.

The force of this was brought home to me by one female client who almost persuaded me that she really never would marry again. Aged precisely thirty-eight, she had fallen in love with her driving instructor at the age of seventeen. A wealthy girl in her own right, her parents had had other plans for her, but she had a strong personality and duly married her man. Four children and years of sustained misery later, she came to me for a divorce. The only real issue was money. The husband made claims on her fortune. The decree was granted but the proceedings dragged on for some while.

Long enough, despite all her protestations that this would never happen, for the lady to have married again. A spree ensued, a new home, motorbikes, a Porsche, an aeroplane, all bought by the new husband with her money.

When we won her case against the first husband, the second husband bought a magnum of champagne to celebrate – again at her expense. He was exactly the same type as her first husband, but very much worse: he went through her money and then abandoned her.

The lesson, of course, is obvious. Do not repeat the mistakes of your first marriage in your second. Perfect sense, but not to do so seems to go against all human urges. For individuals do appear to be attracted to a specific type and a bad experience seldom deters anyone from getting involved with the same type again. Why? A desire to wipe the slate clean again by replaying the first marriage without the mistakes? A need to link up with a particular kind of personality for reasons buried in our psyches? An interesting question for which there are no answers here. Nevertheless, a question to ask yourself when contemplating re-marriage.

38
NEVER?

'Meanwhile time is flying, flying never to return.'
VIRGIL: *Georgics* iii

YOU ONLY LIVE once but you live long enough to learn that in this life, anything is possible. Anything. Two people fall madly in love. They marry 'till death do us part'. But before death, divorce intervenes. By then their love is long departed. Bitter hostility arises between them. It sets hard into the personality affecting all thoughts, all actions, changing your attitude to life. It is like the child pulling an ugly face in the fairy story. When the wind changes, the face becomes fixed forever.

Sometimes, because the parties were once close, this is inevitable. They have fallen from Heaven. Disillusion, hurt, humiliation, have been endured. The sense of loss is bottomless. Deep inside, they have a feeling of desecration. It travels with them wherever they go, even into their next marriage.

What does it signify? In these days, when Republicans and Unionists can hold their fire and Arab can talk to Jew; when Americans can visit Vietnam on vacation; why, just because once they were married, can two people not behave towards each other in a calm and civilized manner? Are they still fighting that same war? Did hostilities not cease with the dissolution of their marriage? What are they trying to achieve? What do they seek to avoid?

Remember anything is possible. Bitterness is like an acid, it burns up all that it touches. Grief is a necessary and legitimate emotion yet even that dissolves with time. If life is to carry on, particularly with a new relationship or marriage, is it not appropriate to bury the past, to let go? For in a strange and wounding way, a continuing loathing for a former spouse is a refusal to give up, to consign the experience of that marriage to history.

It is not just for you that you should allow your passions to mellow, although the advantages of being able to relax, to look at your past with equanimity, to move forward with confidence and actually enjoy the present, must be obvious. It is in relation to those others whom your life touches that an effort should be made.

The incidence of divorce among those whose parents have divorced is far higher than the national average. Your children will have a far better chance of adjusting to your divorce, and developing into rounded adults, if they are not expected to take sides.

Peace. It can be more than that if given a chance. Sometimes relations between former spouses improve when they re-marry. If you have not re-married, ask yourself would it make any difference? If the answer is no, then think hard before re-marrying in case the weight of the emotional baggage is too heavy and sinks the ship. If the answer is yes, then ask yourself why? Pride? There is nothing so terrible about pride, though standing on it will make you no taller. But on its own, it is an insufficient reason to ruin your prospects and your perspective on life.

To thine own self be true. In the end you have only yourself to answer to. All too often, there is a kind of reciprocity to bad feelings. A harsh word in anger engenders an unkind response. Bitterness feeds off itself and relations spiral out of control. It becomes a vicious circle. Sometimes it takes a bold step to stop it – the Israelis talking to the Palestinians – and then, anything is possible.

Be selfish. Would it not be better if you could rationalize the reason for the failure of your marriage; take it out, live with it, and, with the agreement of your former spouse, share with them the responsibility for that failure? Would life not feel a little less harsh if that source of hurt were removed; if it were possible, even only for the sake of the children, to talk to your former spouse without rancour or upset?

Remember positive thinking? Remember the need to keep things in perspective? They apply just as much after the divorce as during it. You have to let go before reaching for the future. Positive thinking and a sense of perspective could just help you do that.

SECTION ELEVEN

❖

INTERESTING CASES

39
ALWAYS

'In all the woes that curse our race
There is a lady in the case.'
W. S. GILBERT: *Fallen Fairies*

*I*N DIVORCE, PROBABLY more than in any other branch of the law, all cases are interesting to the Practitioner. Although over a time and with experience, it is tempting to conclude that one has seen it all before, that each case is merely a variation that will ultimately conform to one of several stereotypes, in fact each case is as individual as the two people who are divorcing.

For if the circumstances giving rise to the divorce may appear commonplace, the reactions of the protagonists to those circumstances will be peculiar to each. Whatever their temperament, divorce will be an emotional experience. Whether a decorated Major General or the first female General Manager of a clearing bank, each of the divorcing couple will be at their most vulnerable. The more demanding the case becomes, the more apparent this will be.

Inevitably, the divorce involves a degree of soul baring, certainly a disclosure of personal problems which in the ordinary course might never be revealed to anyone, let alone to a lawyer. In consequence, the solicitor assumes a high degree of responsibility, aware that the manner in which the case is handled may and probably will have a lasting effect on the client's future. But, more than this, the solicitor will be aware of issues and difficulties which the client will never even have anticipated. It is against these matters particularly that the solicitor's conduct of the case will fall to be judged.

The solicitor and client will go through an immense amount together. In the process, the solicitor will get to know the client extremely well. The resultant relationship will be as fulfilling for the solicitor as any that a lawyer in the other specialities is likely to have. In many ways, the client's life is in the solicitor's hands. This alone should bring out the best in the solicitor.

A professional involvement in a client's problems provides a tremendous insight into life. The cases which I have found most interesting are those where I felt that I learned from the client's experience, often from their example. A short summary of a few such cases follows. These were particularly interesting to me.

1. *Five years' Separation*: I acted for the wife in this case. Married to a high ranking officer in the armed forces, she had four children and a beautiful home. She adored her husband, who was often away on duty. Had anyone asked her, she would have said she was blissfully happy. Love is blind. She had no idea that her husband was involved with another woman. When he told her and asked for a divorce, she was devastated. Her first concern was for her family. All she could focus on was the break-up of her family. She regarded the children and their welfare as of far greater importance than anything else. Gradually, she came to terms with the fact that her marriage was over. Despite the pain and sorrow she bore her husband no malice but she stead-fastly refused to agree to a divorce, even when told that the new lady was carrying the husband's child. The reason was that she believed in her marriage. She wanted her children to see that she would never give it up lightly. The husband

exerted heavy pressure to obtain a divorce. The delay was harming his prospects of further promotion but his wife did not relent. After a period of five years apart, the divorce went ahead. The children remained on good terms with both parents. Now grown up, they are all exceptional people, but none of them have married.

2. *Right is Might*: Another service divorce, where again I was acting for the wife. The issue here was financial. The wife was the petitioner, the husband already living with another woman. He planned to leave the services and go into business, buying and selling pictures. He intended to finance this from his severance payment. He acknowledged that the new business would provide neither the security nor the income needed for him to support his wife and children but he was not prepared to look for a regular job. It was agreed that the fairest solution would be to have a clean break but the husband was at first unwilling to fund this adequately, as he wanted to use his money in the business. The husband wanted to have his cake and eat it. A stalemate ensued. Immense pressure was exerted on the wife both by the husband and his solicitor to persuade her to accept their proposals. The wife and I took the view that without proper provision, she would never be able to make ends meet, to afford to buy even a pair of winter boots. We stuck out for a fair settlement. Time resolved the deadlock. In the end the husband relented and right was done. I still receive a card each year at Christmas, referring to the boots.

3. *Right is Wrong*: I had one case for a husband who was much in the public eye. His wife threw him out for his infidelities, which had been widely reported. He was desolated. He asked me to write to the wife's solicitor, pleading that she change her mind. He asked for one more chance.

The letters were very persuasive but they failed to persuade the wife. The husband was so dismayed that we asked the solicitor to confirm that the wife had seen the letters. They said she had.

The case was settled well from a financial point of view. When it came to the children, the wife's solicitor stipulated that the husband could only see them in the presence of their nanny, whose influence in the family was very considerable. This seemed to me to be the last straw for a man who had so regretted his divorce. Without waiting for instructions, I took a high moral tone, saying how disgraceful it was to presume to step between a man and his children, assuring them that he was able to look after them as well as the next man.

The other side conceded. I reported to the husband, expecting him to be pleased, but it turned out that he would have far preferred to see his children in the company of their nanny. He had never changed a nappy in his life!

4. *Changing the Law*: This case remains a favourite of mine, not because we changed the law but because of a unique double achievement that I suspect is unlikely ever to be repeated.

My client was a French Marquis. On the day in question, I was applying on his behalf to the House of Lords for leave to appeal a judgement from the Court of Appeal. Because of this, I had to turn down an invitation to join some accountant friends of mine in their marquee, to watch a Test Match. So, on the same day, because I went to the Lords for the Marquis, I could not go to the marquee at Lord's!

The point of law was fascinating. The French husband had applied to stay his French wife's proceedings in this country, as he had commenced his own in France where he stood to do better financially. The issue was about conflicting jurisdictions. The only relevant authorities involved shipping cases. These were applied by the Court of Appeal but, in the end, we persuaded the Judicial Committee of the House of Lords to accept that a child was not a ship. Those authorities could not therefore be sensibly applied to his upbringing, as his welfare would not be served by conflicting orders in different jurisdictions. The law was accordingly changed.

5. *Too much Kindness*: One wife I acted for seemed to love her husband too much. In the end, it drove him away and broke up the marriage.

Her problem began when her child was born. Apparently, during labour she was left alone in a bed almost next door to the morgue. Complications set in and she was given a Caesarean. When she came round, everyone was too busy to tell her about her baby. She thought it was dead and suffered terrible shock.

In fact it was a healthy boy but she was told too late and she went into depression from which she never properly emerged. Over the years she underwent various therapies, including electric shock treatment. It seemed that the one thing that kept her going was the way she adored her husband. This proved too heavy a burden for him. He was away a good deal on business and ultimately found someone else.

The wife suffered badly from the divorce. Her health deteriorated further but, as time went by, she too found someone else and began to pull herself together. Then one day a letter arrived on my desk from the husband's solicitors. It asked that the wife desist from entering the husband's new home. Apparently she had filled up his fridge in anticipation of his return from holiday with his new wife.

6. *Too little Kindness*: It is rarely possible to see with one's own eyes exactly what it is that a client has to endure in an unpleasant divorce. When this happens, one inevitably puts oneself in the client's position. Only then does the agony that the client has had to put up with reveal itself in all its force.

Unless there has been a round-table meeting, it is normally necessary to wait for a trial before seeing the spouse in the flesh. In one such case I was acting for a husband. His wife had plainly loved him too little. She turned out to be just as cold, ruthless and manipulative as he had described. Perhaps because conduct was not an issue in the case, and the husband was not the easiest of men to deal with, I had taken much of what he had said about her with a pinch of salt. However, on seeing the lady in court, I understood everything.

The wife had already re-married. The issue to be tried concerned finances for the children. The wife had her own successful business and was also supported by her wealthy new husband. However, even though my client was experiencing hard times, she wanted the children's provision to be increased. Her application was without merit. It was impossible to settle, so we went to court wondering what it was she could possibly be hoping to achieve.

We found out the day before the court hearing. The husband told me that, when his daughter was eight, his wife had accused him of touching the child improperly during a swim. The husband denied that he had done anything of the kind but the wife had made a huge fuss, involving the daughter who had been unaware that anything had happened. The issue had nothing to do with the wife's application but she informed my client that she intended to raise it in court.

There was nothing we could do to stop her. By the time

it came for her to give evidence, the tension was palpable. The wife had everyone's full attention. She looked at the husband with eyes full of hate. Then, inexplicably to the Judge, she broke down. The court adjourned for her to compose herself. When she came back, she had nothing to say. She lost her application and had to pay her ex-husband's costs.

7. *Long Memories*: As every divorcing couple will know, being married is not the same as being happy. But it still seems strange to me when people who have been married for over forty years come to divorce.

With their children long since married, with a clutch of grandchildren and financially secure, what is it that determines a couple to split up? Each case, of course, is different, but I suspect that underlying many of them is the recognition that, with old age coming up over the next hill, this is the last chance to make a break for it, to take a final lunge at life. It must be like the familiar crisis of middle age, though more poignant for now this really is the last chance; it is do or die.

When these marriages break up, the lid comes well and truly off. All manner of allegations and resentments bubble up to the surface and, in a remarkably short space of time, two solid, staid, respectable grandparents have abandoned their image in favour of combat. When battle is drawn the hostilities would not shame Elizabeth Taylor and Richard Burton in *Who's Afraid of Virginia Woolf?*

Two cases stick out. In one, I acted for the husband, in the other for the wife.

In the first the husband saw himself as the victim. Mystified, he simply did not know what had come over his wife. He had no idea what it was that he had done wrong and even the divorce petition did little to enlighten him, as it alleged things such as the husband's misrepresenting his rank when the couple first met during the Second World War, which, if true, had been cleared up a life-time ago.

Always concerned for his wife throughout the proceedings, the husband behaved like a gentleman. In the end, after the matrimonial home had been sold and two new properties bought, the wife took him back. It is strange but neither in this case, nor the one that follows, were the grown-up children of the marriage able to exert much influence to help the parties sort things out.

My other case was a real fight to the death. Once the gloves were off there was no holding the parties back, even though the husband was in his mid-eighties and the wife only ten years younger.

Both parties were larger than life. Each was probably charming on their own but, quite obviously, they were and always had been hopelessly mismatched. The husband deeply resented the wife having the use of his second house or any of his furniture. He gave the impression that he had married beneath him and yet the wife accused him of taking up with 'pub droppings' and became suspicious (rightly, as it turned out) of a nurse who attended to him. The accusations and antics of the parties did credit to neither side. Their proceedings unleashed a flood of venom and ill-will which provided the parties a second wind. They thrived on it, so much so that even driving his car under a lorry, suffering multiple injuries, barely slowed the husband down.

It is easy to say that they would have been better off divorcing years earlier. Maybe they saw the light too late but, equally, perhaps they had always needed each other to spark off. But once the genie was out of the bottle, old age made it impossible to put it back again.

8. *Wisdom*: Parties sometimes get themselves so geared up for a major confrontation, that it proves very difficult to dissuade them from going ahead with their day in court, even when they understand it is not cost effective to do so.

In one case like that, a great deal of money was involved with accountants, valuers and expert witnesses on either side. The husband had diverse assets. He was a very wealthy man. The extent of that wealth was disputed but enough had been disclosed. How it should be split between them was, however, the issue. Try as they may, none of the experts could come up with a solution to satisfy both sides.

The wife did not trust the husband and neither of them would compromise, despite advice that the costs of the case going to trial would be enough to fund a generous settlement on its own.

The hearing date duly arrived. Trolleys full of box files were wheeled into court. The case began. No-one seemed in a particular hurry. The lawyers arranged their books and papers, settling themselves in for a lengthy stay. Timetables for the duration of the hearing and the calling of witnesses were agreed, both sides appearing to be getting on very well. Both sides, that is, except the parties themselves who would hardly look at each other.

But neither the husband nor the wife could have failed to notice how cosy the atmosphere appeared to be. Perhaps it was this which brought the matter to a head. For, during the adjournment for lunch, the husband spoke to the wife. What if he divided the property up by value so that she had one half? The wife was my client. She knew her husband well. Even though she had been prepared to settle for less, she kept her cool. Subject to my advice, she said that she would agree provided that once the husband had made his division, she could choose which half she wanted!

Inadvertently she had stumbled on an old and foolproof Chinese device for the resolution of family disputes. The husband was clearly taken aback. His lawyers were furious that he had offered such terms but he still agreed the deal. Whatever extra money he gave away was covered by the costs that he had saved in not fighting on. His consolation? The money had gone to his wife, not the lawyers.

9. *Alcoholism*: Drink can be the lover, the mistress, the demon who arrives in a home uninvited, settles in unseen, and stays. Voracious, demanding, destabilizing, expensive, before long alcohol has taken over the family. Dominant, reckless, destructive, it becomes a principal player in the marriage. Regarded as an illness, it quickly develops into a kind of torture, subverting all family relationships. Personalities change. Is the husband or the wife the victim? Can anything be done?

Only once have I seen a spouse cure himself in those tragic circumstances. He came to see me at the end of his tether. A confirmed alcoholic, the man really loved his wife but she had made it clear that she would divorce him if he could not mend his ways. He had tried many times before but had never quite succeeded. We talked at length. It was clear that he understood the gravity of his position. His wife, or drink: he could no longer have both. He cut a pathetic figure, in genuine need of help. I sent him to a psychiatrist colleague. A miracle occurred. The man was cured. Seeing him later, I could not believe that it was the same man. He had shown the most tremendous resources of strength and determination to save his marriage and he got his reward.

This was my only experience of alcoholism in marriage to have had a happy ending.

SECTION TWELVE

❖

CONCLUSION

40
NEVER, NEVER, NEVER

'If a man will begin with certainties, he shall end in doubts; but if he will be content to begin with doubts, he shall end in certainties.'

FRANCIS BACON: *Advancement of Learning*

THERE IS ONE final case that I should mention. It embodies many of the principles we have discussed, so I have kept it till last. It also bears a moral as relevant and important as any in this book.

The case concerns a husband for whom I acted, whose wife was divorcing him. She seemed set on making his life a living hell. A successful business man, he found himself thrown out of the matrimonial home, restricted in his access to his only child, and the subject of an increasing barrage of unreasonable demands from his wife. The divorce proceedings affected him very badly. Lost and unable to come to terms with what was happening, he was very deeply hurt.

Then, one frosty winter's morning, everything changed. His wife was driving the child to school. Her car skidded on the ice and crashed. It was unreal. The wife was killed instantly but the child escaped unhurt. In the intake of a single gasp, all was over.

The husband was a decent man. He probably grieved for his wife, even though she had traumatized him, taking every opportunity to cause him anguish. Her conduct had been gratuitous but, in the end, it had served no purpose. Had she been spared, she would have gained nothing from it that she would not have been entitled to, in any event, except, that is, an embittered former husband and a child who was disturbed.

Death is the ultimate leveller, and, as such, an occasional reference to it may be the most effective way to restore one's perspective. Many people in divorce proceedings calculate that their problems would be over if their spouse ceased to exist. They do not thereby desire the death of their spouse. When such a death comes as a relief, there must be something very wrong indeed with the way in which the divorce has been allowed to proceed.

Ask yourself how you would feel. It is a very useful test. Things should never be that bitter, or hopeless or unfair, that the unexpected death of a marriage partner may be regarded as other than tragic. Whilst divorce may certainly bring the worst out in some people, it is simply not about destruction. It is, or should be, merely a civilized way of dissolving the ties that bind two individuals together in marriage.

Remember that, when you go wrong. Never stop reaching. Never take your eye off your goal.

- ALWAYS BE POSITIVE.
- ALWAYS KEEP MATTERS IN PERSPECTIVE.
- ALWAYS PUT THE BEST INTERESTS OF CHILDREN FIRST.
- ALWAYS PLAY BY THE RULES.
- ALWAYS TRY TO AVOID THE PITFALLS DESCRIBED IN THIS BOOK.

Do all of this and you will find that you will emerge in better shape from your divorce than when you went in. That does not mean that divorce is good for you. But it can be managed to ensure that you come out of it whole and purposeful, ready to take up life again.

I have repeated below the table which appears at the start of this book. Why not consider it again, then compare your answers?

Why am I divorcing or thinking about divorce?

How do I feel about my divorce?

What do I expect the outcome to be?

Why?

Aspects of my divorce that worry me.

What should I aim for after my divorce?

Hope springs eternal in the human breast.
Never lose it.

CONCILIATION SERVICES, MEDIATION AND OTHER HELP

1. Family Mediators Association (FMA)
   The Old House
   Rectory Gardens
   Henbury
   Bristol BS10 7AQ
   Telephone: 0117–950–0140
   London Office: 0181–954–6383

The FMA pairs experienced lawyers with qualified professionals expert in counselling or in family work, to provide the specialist skills of trained mediators.

2. National Family Mediation (NFM)
   9 Tavistock Place
   London WC1H 9SN
   Telephone: 0171–383–5993
   See also Appendix III

Formerly the National Family Conciliation Council, NFM specializes in arrangements for children. Most family conciliation services are affiliated to the NFM. The address of your nearest service is available locally through your solicitor or Citizens' Advice Bureau.

3. Divorce Mediation and Counselling Service (DMCS)
   38 Ebury Street
   London SW1W 0LU
   Telephone: 0171–730–2422

DMCS offers counselling services for people who are considering separating. They work on the basis that arrangements made voluntarily between parties, particularly in relation to children, stand a better chance of working if not imposed by the courts.

4. The National Council for One Parent Families
   255 Kentish Town Road
   London NW5 2LX
   Telephone: 0171–267–1361

Works to help parents looking after children on their own. Booklets are issued free to lone parents.

5. Relate (Relate National Marriage Council)
   Herbert Gray College
   Little Church Street
   Rugby
   Warwickshire CV21 3AP
   Telephone: 01788–573241

Formerly Marriage Guidance Council. Local branches are listed in the telephone directory.

6. Jewish Marriage Council
   23 Ravenshurst Avenue
   London NW4 4EE
   Telephone: 0181–203–6311

7. Catholic Marriage Care
   Clitheroe House
   1 Blythe Mews
   Blythe Road
   London W14 0NW
   Telephone: 0171–371–1341

8. Asian Family Counselling Service
   74 The Avenue
   London W13 8LB
   Telephone: 0181–997–5749

9. The National Stepfamily Association
   Chapel House
   18 Hatton Place

London ECIN 8RU
Telephone: 0171–209–2460
0990 168388: counselling Helpline, weekdays 2.00 pm–5.00 pm;
7.00 pm–10.00 pm
Provides information and support for all members of stepfamilies and those who work with them.

10. Reunite
National Council for Abducted Children
P.O. Box 4
London WCI 3DX
Telephone: 0171–404–8356
A self-help network for parents whose children have been abducted.

11. The Family Welfare Association
501–505 Kingsland Road
London E8 4AU
Telephone: 0171–254–6251
Provides social work and social care services to families and individuals.

12. National Council for the Divorced and Separated
P.O. Box 519
Leicester
Leics LE2 3ZE
Telephone and fax: 0116–270–0595
See also Appendix III
Over 100 branches nationwide provide a venue where people with similar problems can meet.

13. Families Need Fathers
134 Curtain Road
London EC2A 3AR
Telephone: 0171–613–5060
Represents non-residential parents and their children. Concerned

with problems of keeping children and parents in contact after family breakdown. National network, booklets.

14. Both Parents Forever
    39 Cloonmore Avenue
    Orpington
    Kent BR6 9LE
    Telephone: 01689–854343

Provides help to all parents and grandparents involved in divorce, separation and care proceedings and where children have been abducted.

15. Family Mediation Scotland
    127 Rose Street
    South Lane
    Edinburgh EH2 4BB
    Telephone: 0131–220–1610

16. Samaritans
    Alcoholics Anonymous
    Drug Abuse Helpline
    Refuge (crisis line)
    Refer to local telephone directories

17. London Marriage Guidance Council
    76A New Cavendish Street
    London W1M 7LB
    Telephone: 0171–580–1087

London Marriage Guidance Council provides unbiased professional counselling for couples or individual partners before, during or after divorce, through nearly 30 centres throughout the London area.

18. Family Mediation Service at the
    Institute of Family Therapy
    43 New Cavendish Street

London WIM 7RG
Telephone: 0171–935–1651
Provides mediation on all issues which can include consultation with children at the request of both parents. Family counselling also available.

19. One Plus One
    12 New Burlington Street
    London WIX IFF
    Telephone: 0171–734–2020
A marriage and partnership research charity concentrating on research into the causes of marital breakdown, training and information.

LEGAL HELP

1. Solicitors' Family Law Association
   P.O. Box 302
   Orpington
   Kent BR6 8QX
   Telephone: 01689–850227

2. The Family Law Bar Association
   Queen Elizabeth Buildings
   Temple
   London EC4Y 9BS
   Telephone: 0171–797–7837

3. The Law Society
   Legal Practice Information Department
   113 Chancery Lane
   London WC2A 1PL
   Telephone: 0171–242–1222

4. Solicitors' Complaints Bureau
   Victoria Court
   8 Dormer Place
   Leamington Spa CV32 5AE
   Telephone: 01926–820082

5. The Legal Aid Board
   85 Grays Inn Road
   London WC1X 8AA
   Telephone: 0171–813–1000

6. The Scottish Legal Aid Board
   44 Drumsheugh Gardens
   Edinburgh EH3 7SW
   Telephone: 0131–226–7061

7. Incorporated Law Society of Northern Ireland
   Legal Aid Department
   Bedford House
   16–22 Bedford Street
   Belfast BT2 7FL
   Telephone: 01232–246441

8. Courts Family Division
   Principal Registry
   Somerset House
   Strand
   London WC2R 1LP
   Telephone: 0171–936–6000

9. Citizens' Advice Bureaux
   See local telephone directory

10. The Law Society of Scotland
    26 Drumsheugh Gardens
    Edinburgh EH3 7YR
    Telephone: 0131–226–7411

11. The Incorporated Law Society of Northern Ireland
    106 Victoria Street
    Belfast BT1 3J2
    Telephone: 01232–231614

PRACTICAL SERVICES

NATIONAL ASSOCIATION OF FAMILY MEDIATION
AND CONCILIATION SERVICES

NFM is an Association of 66 Family Mediation Services in England, Wales and Northern Ireland.

Family mediation is a decision-making process in which an impartial mediator assists the separating or divorcing couple to reach their own mutually agreed solutions to the issues created by separation or divorce.

NFM mediators focus parents on the needs of their children. 70% agree arrangements for their children, who may be directly consulted. Research establishes that mediation reduces bitterness and improves communication, thus benefiting children.

Increasingly NFM mediators mediate issues of finance and property. Of that smaller number, 80% reach agreement. (Joseph Rowntree Foundation Research, 1994.)

Each FMS is a separate charity whose funds are drawn from client fees, the Local Authority, the Probation Service, some Childrens' Charities (NCH Action for Children and Barnardo's), Trusts and Charities and from small legal aid disbursements for reports given to solicitors about the outcomes of the mediation of their legally aided clients.

Charitable status ensures that no family is denied mediation because of lack of money. Subsidy is for those who cannot pay. Fees are charged to those who can.

NFM sets and maintains high standards; NFM, with the Family Mediators Association and Family Mediation Scotland has formed a UK College of Family Mediators.

NFM has 700 mediators, whom it has selected and trained and whom it accredits. Mediators are supervised in their local Services. If paid at a proper professional rate, they could do more work.

NFM Services mediated 6,500 couples in 1994. Some mediate 15–20% of divorcing couples in their area.

80% of couples currently approaching NFM are already separated. 19% of couples currently approaching NFM are not married. If mediated earlier more couples might decide to stay together.

Costs – £25 per person per session or a lower subsidized fee. For All Issues Mediation this is likely to be £600 *per couple*.

Further details from National Family Mediation, 9 Tavistock Place, London WC1H 9SN. Tel: 0171–383–5993; fax: 0171–383–5994.

NATIONAL COUNCIL FOR THE
DIVORCED AND SEPARATED

The National Council for the Divorced and Separated was formed in March 1974 and is a voluntary organization controlled by the Executive Committee, all of whom are prepared to devote their time to helping others. It has branches throughout the British Isles and aims to have a branch in every major town.

NCDS encourage people to join their nearest branch, but where this is not possible membership of the national organization is still available and they are happy to assist in the setting up of new branches. Although primarily interested in promoting an active social life for members, the NCDS can provide general help and support to divorced and separated people through their charitable arm, a registered charity called the NCDS Trust, details of which can be sent on request.

Membership of NCDS is available to all divorced and separated people who provide proof of status. Associate membership may be available to other applicants at the discretion of the local branch committee. There is an annual subscription fee and usually a small admission charge to events. NCDS is a non profit-making organization and aims to provide a social life within the financial reach of everyone.

Members receive *NCDS News*, a quarterly publication which

features up-to-date information and provides space for the members to air their views.

NCDS, whilst supporting re-marriage of divorced persons, which happily occurs from time to time throughout the organization, wish to make it clear that it is not in any way connected with any marriage bureau.

For further details on NCDS organization, please send an SAE to: NCDS, PO Box 519, Leicester, LE2 3ZE. Telephone and fax: 0116–270–0595.

FAMILY LAW ACT 1996 – OUTLINE SUMMARY

After much controversy and passion, both in and out of Parliament, the Family Law Act 1996 received Royal Assent in July 1996.

The Act (which also deals with Pension splitting, Family Homes and Domestic Violence) will change the present divorce process from fault-based divorce to a time-based divorce, the fact that a marriage has broken down irretrievably being demonstrated by the passage of a period of time for reflection and consideration.

The new law is not due to come into effect until 1 January 1999. Until then the old law will continue in force. When the new law is activated its procedures will be very different from those at present.

Taking the view that couples should take responsibility for what has happened to their marriage, and for the consequences of breaking it, there will be no more quickie divorces. The new law will bring an end to marital fault.

The new law will not require one party to prove that the marriage has broken down as a result of the behaviour of the other party or by having lived apart for two or five years. Instead, one or both of the parties has to file a *Statement of Marital Breakdown* recording his, her or their view that the marriage has broken down. Provided that the parties have been married for at least one year, this initiates the marital proceedings with the court. But the divorce process begins before that, when one or both of the parties have attended an *Information Meeting*.

The purpose of this meeting is to provide relevant information about the divorce process. This includes information about marriage support services; the importance of the welfare, wishes and feelings of the children; the type of financial matters which might arise following divorce; the availability of independent legal advice; the divorce process and parties' responsibilities and rights under it;

the availability and advantages of mediation. In addition the parties will be encouraged to have a meeting with a marriage counsellor.

At the end of the *Information Meeting* one or both parties will be given a form of Certification which will enable them, in due course, to proceed to the next stage. This, however, may only be after a period of three months has first elapsed.

After that, one or both of the parties can file a *Statement of Marital Breakdown* at the Court indicating that they believe the marriage has broken down, understand the purpose of the *Period of Reflection and Consideration* and wish to make arrangements for the future. A divorce file will be opened at the Court Office, and the Court will then be empowered to deal with Applications relating to money, children and domestic violence.

If emergency financial assistance is required during the three month period between the *Information Meeting* and the filing of the *Statement of Marital Breakdown* an Application will have to be made to a Family Proceedings Court or to a County Court for neglect to maintain.

The *Statement of Marital Breakdown* is served by the Court on the opposite party and, fourteen days later, the *Period for Reflection and Consideration* begins. During this time it is intended that the couple should reflect on whether their marriage can be saved, have the opportunity to be reconciled, consider what arrangements regarding finance, property and children should be made for the future.

At the end of the period an application for divorce may be made, accompanied by a declaration that, having reflected on the breakdown of the marriage and considered arrangements for the future, the party or parties making the declaration believe that the marriage cannot be saved.

The minimum period is nine months where there are no children of the family under sixteen years of age and fifteen months where there are. It is during this time that the Court expects the parties to discuss and agree all outstanding issues, particularly those relating to children and finance.

So far as children are concerned it is a specific requirement of the Act that the Court is to have particular regard to 'the conduct of the parties in relation to the upbringing of the child', the importance of regular contact (access), and 'any risk to the child attributable to (i) where the person with whom the child will reside is living, or proposes to live or (ii) any person with whom he proposes to live'.

With regard to financial matters (subject to certain exceptions, for example where the other party cannot be traced or is obstructing the proceedings, or the ill health of either party), the person who filed the *Statement of Marital Breakdown* will have to produce to the Court one of the following:

(a) a Court Order (made by consent or otherwise)

(b) a negotiated agreement

(c) a Declaration by both parties that they have made their financial arrangements

(d) a Declaration by one party (to which the other does not object) that there are no assets, no Applications to be made and no arrangements to be considered.

A Divorce cannot be obtained until the finances and the arrangements for the children have been resolved. In practice this may lead to serious delays, significantly lengthening the divorce process. The *Period for Reflection and Consideration* will therefore be extended until they have. Only then (and after the minimum period has elapsed) may the Applicant apply for and be granted a *Divorce Order*.

Unlike the present system there will be no Decree Nisi. The Order will take immediate effect. It is unlikely that an opposing party could prevent a divorce. To do so they would have to apply to the Court for an Order preventing the divorce on the ground that the dissolution of the marriage would result in substantial financial or other hardship and that it would be wrong in all the circumstances for the marriage to be dissolved. Such an Application would be successful only in the most unusual circumstances.

Adding up all the different time limits, and subject to all matters relating to children and finances being resolved, the minimum period in which a divorce may be obtained is twelve months plus fourteen days where there are no children under sixteen years of age, and eighteen months plus fourteen days where there are.

The guiding principle of the new legislation is that where marriages are brought to an end, this should be done with the minimum of distress to parties and children, so as to encourage the best possible relationships between the parties and the children, and without incurring unreasonable costs.

Both mediation and independent legal advice will be available to the parties. The key to making the new provisions work effectively will be to keep conflict to a minimum.

NEGATIVE FEELINGS

'Are you so in love with sorrow
that you cannot part with part of it?'

JOHN WEBSTER: *The Duchess of Malfi*

How to score:
    −4 for each feeling that you have
    +2 for each feeling that you do not have at present
    +6 when this feeling is no longer a factor.

Recognizing that these feelings have to go is half the battle.

TABLE OF NEGATIVE FEELINGS

	Now	1	2	3	4	5	6	7	8	9	10	11	12
1. Shock													
2. Uncertainty													
3. Denial of reality													
4. Anger													
5. Sadness													
6. Frustration													
7. Resentment													
8. Bitterness													
9. Fear													
10. Insecurity													
11. Jealousy													
12. Guilt													
13. Hatred													
14. Despair													
15. Loneliness													
16. Anxiety													
17. Self-pity													
18. Self-hate													
19. Sense of failure													
20. Desperation													
21. Rejection													
22. Loss of control													
23. Overtaken by problems													
24. Grief													
Total													

As your score increases, you will see that you are coming to terms with your situation. If your score does not improve, you need to work harder. You might like to read this book again.

GOOD LUCK!

---

13 14 15 16 17 18 19 20 21 22 23 24

GLOSSARY

1. *Obtaining a divorce*: The only ground for divorce under the existing law is that the marriage has irretrievably broken down. To prove this, one or more of the following five 'facts' have to be proved:

    (i) the respondent has committed adultery and the petitioner finds it intolerable to live with the respondent;

    (ii) the respondent has behaved in such a way that the petitioner cannot reasonably be expected to live with the respondent;

    (iii) the respondent has deserted the petitioner for at least two years;

    (iv) the parties have lived apart for at least two years, and the respondent consents to a divorce; or

    (v) the parties have lived apart for at least five years.

2. *Adultery*: Voluntary sexual intercourse by a married person with a third party of the opposite sex at any time before decree absolute.

3. *Affidavit*: A written statement on oath containing a person's evidence.

4. *Calderbank Offer*: A letter containing a financial offer, written in advance of a final hearing, which may be produced to the court only on the question of costs.

5. *Clean-break*: An order dealing with all financial issues, capitalizing maintenance payments to bring to an end financial dependence between the parties.

6. *Consent*: The term applied to facts (iv) and (v) to be proved in obtaining a divorce (see 1).

7. *Contact*: An order for a child to visit or stay with the parent with whom the child is not living, or to exchange letters, telephone calls etc. Contact orders may also be made in favour of non-parents (e.g. grandparents).

8. *Decree Absolute*: The order dissolving the marriage.

9. *Desertion*: A period of separation of at least two years brought about by a husband or wife leaving the other against the deserted party's wishes.

10. *Disclosure*: Complete information about all matters relevant to a financial application.

11. *Fault*: The term used to describe any of the first three of the facts to be proved in obtaining a divorce (see 1).

12. *Irretrievable breakdown*: The sole ground for divorce (see 1).

13. *Maintenance payments*: The provision of income support made by one party to the other and/or to the children in a divorce.

14. *Petition*: The application for a divorce.

15. *Petitioner*: The person who commences divorce proceedings by filing the petition.

16. *Residence*: An order which settles the arrangement as to where a child is to live. Normally made in favour of one parent, it may be shared between both; third parties such as grandparents may sometimes apply for residence orders as well.

17. *Respondent*: The petitioner's spouse.

18. *Unreasonable behaviour*: The second of the facts to be proved in obtaining a divorce (see 1).

Under the Family Law Act 1996:

19. *Divorce Order*: An Order dissolving a marriage.

20. *Information Meeting*: Meeting with which divorce process begins, to provide information about the divorce process.

21. *Period for reflection and consideration*: A period commencing fourteen days after the filing of the Statement of Marital Breakdown for the parties to reflect on whether the marriage can be saved and to consider what arrangements should be made for the future.

22. *Statement of marital breakdown*: A statement by one of the parties that the maker of the statement (or each of them) believes that the marriage has broken down.

ACKNOWLEDGEMENTS

Writing this book has brought me many pleasures – encouragement and support from friends and colleagues who read the text and made suggestions, each person, curiously, offering entirely different comments; a host of new friends, many of whom have graciously allowed their names to appear in the book through their endorsements; feedback from readers who have found the book of help. To all these kind people I am much indebted.

I am also very grateful, and not a little proud, to have had Marje Proops add a Foreword to this edition.

Working with Penguin has been a warm and rewarding experience. In Eleo Gordon not only has the book found a staunch friend but, thanks to her insistence, my computer now has a master who (almost) understands it! My best thanks to Eleo, to Margaret Bluman, Sara Marafini, Sue Miles, Penny Daniel, Jenny Dufton, Caroline Sanderson and the entire Penguin team.

Finally to Joey, my wife of nearly twenty years. Well, what can you say in a divorce book about your wife? Far from being put off by my writing a book on this subject, so much did she enjoy each word as I wrote it, she feels this book should become compulsory reading for all married couples. That says it all . . . I think!

INDEX

INDEX

Visit Penguin on the Internet
and browse at your leisure

- preview sample extracts of our forthcoming books
- read about your favourite authors
- investigate over 10,000 titles
- enter one of our literary quizzes
- win some fantastic prizes in our competitions
- e-mail us with your comments and book reviews
- instantly order any Penguin book

and masses more!

'To be recommended without reservation ... a rich and rewarding on-line experience' – Internet Magazine

READ MORE IN PENGUIN

In every corner of the world, on every subject under the sun, Penguin represents quality and variety – the very best in publishing today.

For complete information about books available from Penguin – including Puffins, Penguin Classics and Arkana – and how to order them, write to us at the appropriate address below. Please note that for copyright reasons the selection of books varies from country to country.

In the United Kingdom: Please write to *Dept. EP, Penguin Books Ltd, Bath Road, Harmondsworth, West Drayton, Middlesex UB7 0DA*

In the United States: Please write to *Consumer Sales, Penguin USA, P.O. Box 999, Dept. 17109, Bergenfield, New Jersey 07621-0120*. VISA and MasterCard holders call 1-800-253-6476 to order Penguin titles

In Canada: Please write to *Penguin Books Canada Ltd, 10 Alcorn Avenue, Suite 300, Toronto, Ontario M4V 3B2*

In Australia: Please write to *Penguin Books Australia Ltd, P.O. Box 257, Ringwood, Victoria 3134*

In New Zealand: Please write to *Penguin Books (NZ) Ltd, Private Bag 102902, North Shore Mail Centre, Auckland 10*

In India: Please write to *Penguin Books India Pvt Ltd, 706 Eros Apartments, 56 Nehru Place, New Delhi 110 019*

In the Netherlands: Please write to *Penguin Books Netherlands bv, Postbus 3507, NL-1001 AH Amsterdam*

In Germany: Please write to *Penguin Books Deutschland GmbH, Metzlerstrasse 26, 60594 Frankfurt am Main*

In Spain: Please write to *Penguin Books S. A., Bravo Murillo 19, 1° B, 28015 Madrid*

In Italy: Please write to *Penguin Italia s.r.l., Via Felice Casati 20, I–20124 Milano*

In France: Please write to *Penguin France S. A., 17 rue Lejeune, F–31000 Toulouse*

In Japan: Please write to *Penguin Books Japan, Ishikiribashi Building, 2–5–4, Suido, Bunkyo-ku, Tokyo 112*

In South Africa: Please write to *Longman Penguin Southern Africa (Pty) Ltd, Private Bag X08, Bertsham 2013*